The Language of Children

Dr. **Mathilda Holzman** is an associate professor at Tufts University in Medford, Massachusetts, where she teaches in the Eliot-Pearson Department of Child Study. She holds a Ph.D. from the University of Washington and has written numerous articles on the subject of child development.

The LANGUAGE OF CHILDREN

Development in Home and School

Mathilda Holzman

A SPECTRUM BOOK

Prentice-Hall, Inc., Englewood Cliffs, New Jersey 07632

Library of Congress Cataloging in Publication Data

Holzman, Mathilda.
    The language of children.

    "A Spectrum Book."
    Bibliography: p.
    Includes index.
    1. Children—Language.   2. Language acquisition.
I. Title.
LB1139.L3H64 1983   372.6   83-10921
ISBN 0-13-523027-6
ISBN 0-13-523019-5 (pbk.)

Tables 8.1., 8.2., 8.3., and 8.4. reprinted from Shatz, M., "The relationship between cognitive
processes and the development of communication skills," in Keasy, C.B. (ed)
Nebraska Symposium on Motivation by permission of University of Nebraska Press.
Copyright © 1977 by University of Nebraska Press.

10   9   8   7   6   5   4   3   2   1

ISBN 0-13-523027-6

ISBN 0-13-523019-5 (PBK.)

Editorial/production supervision by Norma G. Ledbetter
Cover design by Hal Siegel
Manufacturing buyer: Christine Johnston

PRENTICE-HALL INTERNATIONAL, INC., *London*
PRENTICE-HALL OF AUSTRALIA PTY. LIMITED, *Sydney*
PRENTICE-HALL CANADA INC., *Toronto*
PRENTICE-HALL OF INDIA PRIVATE LIMITED, *New Delhi*
PRENTICE-HALL OF JAPAN, INC., *Tokyo*
PRENTICE-HALL OF SOUTHEAST ASIA PTE. LTD., *Singapore*
WHITEHALL BOOKS LIMITED, *Wellington, New Zealand*
EDITORA PRENTICE-HALL DO BRASIL LTDA., *Rio de Janeiro*

to my husband, Frank,
for his support and encouragement

and to our children, Tom, David, and Miriam,
from whom the first inklings and glimmerings
for this book came

Contents

Foreword

The study of children's language, perhaps more than any other domain of child study, has been beset by theories. Early on there were the "Bow Wow" and the "Woof Woof" theories that language began as an expression of emotion or as an attempt to copy sounds in the environment. There was Skinner's theory of "mands" and "tacts" and of course Chomsky's theory of generative grammar, which gave birth to many little theories such as "pivot grammar." Indeed, some wag (it may have been George Miller) talked about a "Theory of the Month Club" with respect to the outpourings of those working on children's language.

Now in science a profusion of theory usually occurs in the infancy of a discipline (when there is no data) or in its maturity (when there is too much). Although those working in language development have had some data, it was rarely enough to warrant the amount of theorizing that ensued. Perhaps language, because it has been studied by others such as linguists, grammarians, writers, and so forth, gives the impression of being more systematized, more ready for conceptualization, say, than perceptual development. And yet, factual knowledge about the acquisition, comprehension, and utilization of language is still very scarce even by psychological standards.

These considerations are what make Mathilda Holzman's book so refreshing and so special. She knows the state of her discipline and does not put on unwarranted theoretical airs. She deals mainly with the research, with everyday examples and personal anecdotes, and ties these together around basic themes and issues in contemporary psycholinguistics. She does, of course, bring in theory and hypotheses but of the miniature variety aimed at circumscribed issues. It is a very readable, up-to-date presentation of the field devoid of the grand schemes that have made psycholinguistics suspect to investigators in other fields.

In this book the reader will be presented with a strong foundation in such issues as beginning reading, animal language, and bilingual education. But the reader will also be presented with as many questions as answers and will be challenged to test the observations against his or her own experience. This is a very solid book for beginners, but it has lessons to teach those in the field who are still tempted to go overboard on theory. This is a very empirical book and it is just what students and the discipline need.

DAVID ELKIND, Ph.D.

Preface

This book provides an introduction to an understanding of the human child's development of language use. The use of language is a basic and dominant feature of human behavior. Some would say language use is the source from which the unique qualities of the human species derive. In this book the development of language use by human beings is related to the development of signaling by other animal species and to the early history of the human child as infant in interaction with his or her mother (or other caretaker). The child's development as a language user after early childhood is related to cognitive development, schooling, and social experience outside the family circle. The consideration of language use development as it relates to the range of experiences that influence it makes the book useful to developmental psychologists, early childhood education specialists, and persons concerned with reading, second language learning, and other topics in addition to the initial development of language by the preschool child.

Beside the college undergraduate and professionals mentioned above, this book will be of interest to the parent who becomes interested in the development of language use from observing his or her own child become a language user. The book assumes no previous knowledge of the subject on the part of the reader.

The manuscript was largely written while I was a visiting scholar at the Center for Applied Linguistics, which turned out to be an excellent (and interesting) environment for writing. My colleagues at the Center discussed issues with me, suggested material for me to read, and read and criticized drafts of chapters—to my great benefit. Donna Christian, Dora Johnson, James Bauman, Russell Campbell, and Walt Wolfram of the Center, Judith Orasanu of the National Institute of Education, Barbara Finkelstein of the School of Education, University of Maryland, Peter Temin of MIT, and

Camille Haneon of Connecticut College all helped me substantially with comments and criticism. Drawings of the illustrations for the book were done by Miriam Holzman, and I thank her. Kristina Mortensen, Sonia Kundert, and Tillie Nelder typed and patiently retyped the manuscript, and I thank them.

Grateful acknowledgment is given to the following for granting permission to reprint material.

Figure 3.1. From R. Herrnstein, D. Loveland, and C. Cable, "Natural concepts in pigeons," *Journal of Experimental Psychology, Animal Behavior Processes,* vol. 2, no. 4, 285-311. Copyright © 1976 by the American Psychological Association. Reprinted by permission of the author.

Excerpt from *Psycholinguistics* by Roger Brown. Copyright © 1970 by The Free Press, a Division of Macmillan Publishing Co., Inc.

Table 7.6. From Terrace, H., et al. "Can an ape create a sentence," *Science,* 206 (1979), 891-903. Copyright © 1979 by the American Association for the Advancement of Science.

Table 9.1. Based on information from Werner, H., and E. Kaplan, "The acquisition of word meanings: a developmental study," *Monograms of the Society for Research in Child Development,* 15 (1950) p. 4.

Figure 9.3. From "Where is under: from memories of instances to abstract features concepts" by Mathilda Holzman, *Journal of Psycholinguistic Research,* vol. 10, no. 4, 1981. Used by permission of Plenum Publishing Corporation.

The Language of Children

1

Human Beings: Geniuses with Language

This is a book about how human beings, who start out in life able only to cry and coo, become language users. In the late 1960s and early 1970s I used to see in the news magazines a full-page advertisement, featuring a picture of an exotic and winsome four-year-old, captioned, "She speaks fluent Urdu [for example], Why can't you?" This was an advertisement for a foreign language school that specialized in preparing Americans to speak a range of foreign languages fluently so that, when they went to foreign countries, they would be able to converse with the people in their own languages. The advertisement was compelling. Certainly an adult American could learn to do anything a four-year-old child could do—and it shouldn't take very long. This ad hasn't been seen for quite a while. Perhaps it has been banned under the law that prohibits false and misleading advertising. It was certainly misleading. Children are able to learn to speak a language without consulting grammar books or dictionaries. They become fluent in their mother tongue, like the little speaker of Urdu, by the time they are about four years old—and some do so considerably earlier. Furthermore, children who move from their native country to a new country where a new language is spoken will become fluent in less than a year in the new language, learning it from playing with other children and being in school where the new language is the language of instruction. The child will learn to speak the new language without an accent. For the adult, learning a new language is much more problematic, and the weight of evidence suggests that it is impossible for a human being who has not learned any language before puberty ever to learn one.

Because human beings, with very few exceptions, are from an early age masters of the complex behavior that is language use, people are not overly impressed with language use—except for people like me who study it. The mastery of language that four-year-old children display is like Perlman's

1

mastery of the violin. We are geniuses at learning our native language. An eminent psycholinguist (that is, a person who studies language as a psychological as well as linguistic topic) has said, "I have two theories of language development, the miracle theory and the impossible theory." This is a way of saying that we do not understand how mastery of language use is achieved at such an early age. Figuring it out is a tantalizing goal, but thus far no one has produced an account of the process that is convincing to others in the field. The first seven chapters of this book describes what we think we know about this impossible miracle.

THE SIGNAL SYSTEMS OF ANIMALS

In contrast to human beings, other animal species do not have languages; they have signal systems. The chapters to come describe what it means to be the user of a human language and how human language differs from animal signal systems. But first, what are animal signal systems?

Animals in the wild are born with a repertoire of signals, and these are all the signals they will ever use. Signaling behavior is not intentional but is a response, like the alarm cry of the sparrow, that is elicited by a stimulus, like the sight of a hawk flying overhead. The flight of little birds upon hearing the sparrow's alarm cry is, again, not intentional behavior, but an involuntary fear response. Animal signals and the responses evoked in others of their species are stereotyped and few in number. The signal code is the entire set of possible messages. That is, no signals are ever combined to produce a new message.

Animals in contact with human beings (such as pets or experimental animals) learn signals in addition to the innate ones. The additional signals are learned through *conditioning,* a well-known type of learning. (Conditioning is described in Chapter Three as it applies to acquiring signals.) The nature of animal signals, whether innate or acquired through conditioning, is that they are not intentional; therefore, animals do not tell lies since lies are messages delivered with the intention to misinform the receiver.

FROM ANIMAL SIGNAL SYSTEMS
TO HUMAN LANGUAGE

The crying and cooing behavior of very young human, "prelinguistic" infants (the first subject of Chapter Four) is comparable to the signaling behavior of the other animal species in that it is nonintentional. The human newborn appears to have three distinguishable cries coordinated to sensations of pain, hunger, and diffuse sensations of frustration and discomfort.

Infants I have studied (Allen, Carol, Jean, and Joel) in interaction with their mothers began to learn, from as early as ten weeks of age, behaviors that are essential to human language use. They learned the turn-taking rules that make conversation possible; they learned to produce the phonological patterns of English. Their acts of reaching for an object and being unable to get it were shaped into a protolinguistic request gesture. The infants learned to participate in verbal rituals with their mothers that were meaningless to the infants except as social interaction. All this early learning took place before these infants were language users and seems no different in kind from the learning of animals in contact with human beings. The same process, conditioning, is adequate to explain the infants' and the animals' learning. Of course, animals cannot learn English phonology; they do not have the right kind of vocal tract. However, sometime during the second year of life a radical change takes place, and infants begin to be language users as opposed to just involuntary senders and receivers of signals. Words are no longer used solely in rote-learned rituals or as part of a stereotyped request gesture. Infants act as though they have caught on to the verbal dimension of experience. They begin to acquire new words much more rapidly than before. Then they begin to produce utterances consisting of two or several words, rather than just one.

ARE COMPETENT LANGUAGE USERS PREDISPOSED TO TEACH LANGUAGE?

The behavior of the infants when they were producing only one-word utterances elicited word-use reinforcement and teaching responses from their mothers. As the infants emerged from the period in which their utterances were never longer than one word, their mothers' responses to the infants' one-word utterances (of which there continued to be many) changed. Instead of responding with the usual word-use teaching and reinforcement, mothers treated their infants' one-word utterances as ordinary contributions to the conversation. The word-teaching behavior of mothers and its cessation, plus their earlier vocalizing behavior, raises the question of innateness of mothers' language-teaching behavior.

CAN APES SPEAK A HUMAN LANGUAGE?

Like many others, I have been intrigued by the possibility that animals other than humans can acquire human language. After all, Allen, Carol, Jean, and Joel started with the same kind of signaling repertoire as animals in the wild; they learned new communicative responses through conditioning, as do pets and experimental animals in contact with people. It seemed possible that apes, taught human language the way infants are. . . .

Apes do not have the same vocal capacity as human beings to acquire *speech,* but they have the dexterity necessary to acquire a manual language.

Since the late 1960s various apes have been taught the sign language of the deaf, a human language. How has it worked out? In Chapter Six the criteria for human language are described, and in Chapter Seven, the speech of Allen, Carol, Jean, and Joel at two years is analyzed to determine to what extent it conforms to the criteria for human language. Then the comparison is made between these human infants and a chimpanzee, Nim Chimpsky.

WHAT DISTINGUISHES HUMAN LANGUAGE FROM ANIMAL SIGNAL SYSTEMS?

There are three characteristics of language use for human beings' communication that are most important in distinguishing human language from animal signal systems:

1. Human language is productive rather than stereotyped. New messages are constantly produced because words can be, and are, put together in new combinations to produce messages that have not been heard previously. The signals of an animal signal system cannot be combined to produce new messages. Combining words is possible because human language has rules for combining words to form sentences. Knowing the grammar of one's language (the rules) makes it possible for the speaker to produce new messages.

2. In its fully developed form, verbal communication becomes independent of *context;* we are able to understand messages without being able to see what is going on as the verbal communication is made. This is possible because the speaker knows what has to be included in a message to compensate for the hearer's being unable to see the context. This characteristic of human language use makes telephone communication possible, as well as the preservation of knowledge in written form.

3. Language is used by human beings in communicative acts. Animal signals are *informative.* The sparrow's alarm cry informs other birds of danger, but the cry is not communicative because it is an involuntary response to the sensation of fear. The sparrow does not intend to warn the other birds. In human communication the speaker intends to warn the hearer with the message, "Look out!" The message succeeds as a warning because the hearer understands that the speaker said, "Look out!" because the speaker believed the hearer was in danger.

LANGUAGE DEVELOPMENT, COGNITIVE DEVELOPMENT, SCHOOLING, AND SOCIAL EXPERIENCE OUTSIDE THE FAMILY CIRCLE

The first seven chapters of this book deal with the development from animal signal systems to human language. The remaining five chapters are concerned with human language development in relation to cognitive development (development of the mental processes by which knowledge is acquired), schooling, and social experience outside the home and family circle. Chapter Ten deals with reading and how children's general language experiences affect the ease or difficulty with which they learn to read. Since the 1970s there has been extensive consideration of the educational difficulties of some children in American public schools who are not native English speakers. This is one of the social policy problems discussed in Chapter Eleven, "Bilingualism and Second Language Learning."

The topic of Chapter Twelve is sociolinguistics, language as an aspect of social behavior consonant with the other expressions of social values and beliefs. You don't say, "Pick me up a ham sandwich and coffee" to the boss because you can't order the boss around (you never could). As a matter of fact, in the United States in the 1980s teachers say to kindergartners, "Do you want to put the blocks away," or "If we don't hurry and put the blocks away, we'll be late for snack." They don't say, "Put the blocks away," because they do not want to order the children around. Does this confuse children who are used to having their behavior guided by imperatives like, "Put the blocks away"? Do the children think they have a choice when they hear, "Do you want . . ."?

The ways in which sex, age, and social status of speaker and hearer affect language use will be discussed in Chapter Twelve. George Bernard Shaw, the playwright, will be considered a sociolinguist. In *Pygmalion* (upon which the musical *My Fair Lady* is based) Shaw advanced the theory, and provided evidence, that a person is believed to be a member of the social class in whose accents he or she speaks.

In Chapter Twelve there is also some discussion of the ingrained sexism in our language. We are referred to as *mankind* rather than *humankind*; when we want to refer back to a nonspecific person, we use the masculine pronouns, for example, "If a young child is malnourished, *he* will lack energy." I have wrestled with the problem in writing this book, but hopefully have avoided sexist language.

Language development is a scientific topic, and it has not been possible to avoid using scientific or technical terms in this book. I have tried to accompany each first use of a scientific or technical term with a definition, placed in parentheses. At the end of the book there is a glossary of scientific and technical terms.

2

The Signal Systems
of Animals
in the Wild

Why does a book about the development of human language start with a consideration of animals in the wild? It has been thought that human language as it exists today—English, Chinese, Arabic, Turkish, and the many other tongues familiar and unfamiliar to Americans—must have evolved from some more primitive human language. This more primitive human language, people have reasoned, would be like the signal systems of the lower animal species with which this chapter is concerned. Hundreds of human languages have now been studied. Many having a spoken but a not written form have been investigated, including the languages of human societies which have extremely primitive technologies. But nowhere has a human society been found, no matter how primitive its technology, that does not have a developed spoken language based on the principle of combining words according to grammatical rules to form sentences. The beginnings of human language are lost to us as far as we know because, until fairly recently in human history, there were no written languages. When a human society with a spoken language but not a written one dies out, its language dies with it. In the 1950s, I lived in Seattle, Washington and knew anthropologists from the University of Washington who were gathering language samples from elderly informants, members of Northwest Indian tribes on the verge of extinction. The anthropologists were hurrying to get a record before it was too late, before the last remaining speakers of the language died.

Even though it is not possible to investigate the continuity of human language and the signaling systems of the lower animals via a primitive human language, the relationship between animal signals and human language can still be examined. The reason it is of significant interest to me, a psycholinguist, is my conviction that our capacity for language use is the keystone to our human (as distinct from our animal) natures. Out of this conviction comes the curiosity to find out what lines of continuity with other animals' signals can be discovered. Jane Goodall has written a book about chimpanzees she observed living in the wild in Africa. She called this book *In the Shadow of Man*. Her title reflects her conviction that chimpanzees are next in the evolutionary line to man. She discovered tool use and tool-making behaviors, information-transmitting behaviors, and even carniverous behaviors on the part of chimpanzees analogous to human behavior. There are similarities between human and animal behavior that touch and impress us all. Everyone knows of instances of courage, devotion to offspring, and cleverness on the part of various animals. We are impressed with the amazing things that circus animals can be taught to do. And yet, the reason the dog who can ride a bicycle or the horse who seems to count impresses us is that we are aware of the vast difference between animal culture and human culture, culture being understood here as intellectual and artistic activity and products.

The ability to use language is a crucial, maybe *the* crucial, element in human culture. Language use is a powerful and efficient means to share and store information. Although much information can be shared by word of mouth and stored in memory, the development of written language has made it possible to transcend barriers of space and time in transmitting information. In order to think about the relationship of human language to animal signal systems we need to consider animal signals as a means for information transmission and storage in comparison to human languages. We also need to see what can be learned about animal species as communicators compared to human beings.

SIGNALING AND COMMUNICATING

Until now, I have avoided using the word *communication* in talking about the sharing or transmitting of information by animals. I want to be able to preserve the distinction made by J.C. Marshall (1970) between informative behavior and communicative behavior. My frequently spilling my glass of water at the dinner table would inform others of the fact that I am clumsy. But unless I intended my action to inform, it is not communicative behavior. Current research indicates that the signaling behavior of animals in the wild is informative but not communicative. The alarm cry of the sparrow emitted as a hawk flies overhead causes other birds and animals that fall prey to marauding birds to flee or seek cover. The flight behavior is part of an innate coordination, the stimulus for which is the alarm cry. But the alarm cry is not an intentional warning like "watch out" uttered by one boy to the other boys in the street as he sees the neighborhood bully approaching from around a corner.

Instead, the alarm cry of the sparrow is also part of an innate coordination; in this case the cry is a response to an environmental stimulus.

The sight of the hawk causes a sensation of fright in the sparrow, which always results in the sparrow's emitting an alarm cry. Human beings also have innate coordinations of this sort. If someone were to sneak up behind you and jab you with a pin, you would emit a noise of discomfort. The noise would be involuntary, caused by the unexpected painful jab. Anyone within earshot would be informed that you had been hurt, even though your cry was not intended. In terms of the definitions of this chapter your cry would be informative but not intentional and therefore not communicative.

Most human vocalizations are intended, but animal signals—both vocal and visual—are involuntary, part of an innate coordination.[1] The animal cannot help emitting the signal. It is caused by the sensation in the animal evoked by the external stimulus. A secondary ground for accepting the innate coordination explanation for the sparrow's alarm cry, rather than an explanation based on the sparrow's intending to warn the other birds, stems from Lloyd Morgan's canon of parsimony. This is the principle that one should attribute to an organism no more intelligence, consciousness, or rationality than will suffice to account for its behavior.

THE SIGN STIMULUS

Following Tinbergen (1951), cited by Marshall (1970), ethologists have distinguished informative exchanges among members of animal species from other regular behavior patterns by means of the sign stimulus concept. A sign stimulus is part of an animal's appearance or behavioral repertoire, which includes vocalizations, that reliably elicits a particular type of response from another animal of the same species. The primary function of sign stimuli is to elicit behavior that ensures the continuation of the species. Sign stimuli have evolved, then, as specific *releasers* of adaptive behavior patterns. The theory is that species with innate signaling coordinations in their repertoires which serve to ensure continuation of the species in its environment of biological adaptation have greater survival potential than other species. Evidence for the theory comes from demonstrating, in a range of cases, what the sign stimulus is. This involves presenting, by itself, the behavior or part of the animals appearance that is the sign stimulus candidate to see if it will evoke the expected, adaptive response. The technique has been successfully exploited by N. Tinbergen, Konrad Lorenz, Edward Ohreson, P. Marler, and many others in isolating sign stimuli for adaptive responses in insects, fish, birds, and mammals (Marshall 1970).

Playing the sparrow's alarm cry on a remote controlled tape recorder near an area where sparrows are feeding is an example of the technique. If the

---

[1]In the last part of this chapter, I will discuss birdsong, which, in some species, contains learned elements. Those elements do not interfere with birdsong's being one part of an innate coordination. Rather, elements that the chicks hear in the adult male song are learned by imitation and become incorporated in the chicks' song, making it possible to identify family members.

recorded cry causes the sparrows to fly away (the adaptive response), then the alarm cry is a sign stimulus. This procedure does *not* prove that the sparrow, when it gives the alarm cry, does not intend to warn the other sparrows. But making the assumption that the alarm cry is a specific releaser, or an innate, involuntary behavior, places the burden of proof on those who claim that the informative behaviors of animals in the wild are intentional. The best way to prove that informative behavior on the part of animals is intentional would be to demonstrate an intention to misinform, in other words, to present examples of animals lying. Thus far, no scientifically acceptable evidence of animals in the wild intentionally misinforming other animals has been produced. The well known behavior of low nesting birds like the bobwhite, which involves the bird's hopping away from its nest, dragging a wing as though it were broken, is an innate response to a predator's approaching the nest. It looks of course as though the bobwhite is pretending its wing is broken to deceive the predator into following it instead of heading for the baby birds in the nest.

Although I say animals don't lie, I am always being given examples of misinforming behavior on the part of people's pets or animals seen in zoos. Actually, I used to attribute an intention to misinform to the dogs in our neighborhood who, in play with other dogs, growl, chase, and jump on each other. They are pretending aggressive behavior, and this seems like possible intentional behavior. One prominent piece of behavior I had observed in these "pretend" fights is a little jump, ending with the dog crouched on its forelegs and standing on its hindlegs. It turns out that this is called a *playbow* and evidence for its "evolution as a stereotyped mammalian display" has been reported (Berkoff 1977). It is a sign stimulus signaling that what follows is play. It is highly stereotyped behavior that has been observed in infant coyotes, infant wolves, infant wolf-malamute hybrids, and domestic dogs. There are no important differences in bows performed by infants of different ages and the first bows performed by pups who were hand reared and had never interacted with another animal or seen a bow. The playbow fulfills the requirements for a sign stimulus, making it possible for canines to play at aggression. We do not know why such play is adaptive behavior for coyotes, wolves, and dogs. It is clear that playing is more adaptive than real fighting, but the function of interaction among animals of the same species for other than mating, hunting, or other survival-serving behaviors is not clear.

RITUALIZATION

A signal or sign stimulus indicating that an animal's behavior is sexual rather than aggressive is certainly adaptive. The displays that signal sexual readiness must be quite clear so that they do not signal aggressiveness. The concept of ritualization, originated by Julian Huxley, is used to explain the evolution of displays that are clear indicators of sexual readiness to species members, even though difficult for human investigators to interpret. E. O. Wilson (1972) has described the ritualization of the dance fly's courtship behavior. Dance flies are carnivorous species classified together as the family, *Empididae.* Many of the species engage in a courtship in which the male makes a simple approach to the female after which copulation takes place. Among other species the male first captures an insect and presents it to the female before copulation. This appears to reduce the chance that the female will eat the male instead of copulating with it. In still other species, the male attaches threads of silk to the insect he is presenting to the female. This makes his offering more distinctive in appearance, a step toward ritualization. Further steps can be observed in other dance flies. In one species the male wraps his offering in a silk sheet. In another, the size of the insect presented to the female is reduced, but the wrapping is such that it does not appear to be partially empty. The male of another species does not bother to catch an insect and presents an empty silken wrapping to the female. This last behavior would be very hard for scientists to interpret if the other species of the dance fly did not exist so that the ritualization of the male's behavior could be observed.

CHEMICAL SIGNALS

Chemical signals called pheromones are involved in the social behavior of many animals. Anyone who has had a dog for a pet is aware of the importance of pheromones (smells) in the social life of the dog. E.O. Wilson has demonstrated that the social life of insects is mediated largely by pheromones. He studied a type of ant whose behavior evoked a feeling of fellowship in entomologists (persons who study insects). Those ants bury their dead. They do not exactly bury, but they carry dead ants to a spot somewhat removed from the ant hill. Wilson was able to demonstrate that the sign stimulus for the burying behavior was a pheromone given off by dead ants. He smeared a lively ant with the candidate pheromone, and shortly after two ants picked up the lively ant and carried him to the burial spot. They put the lively ant down, and he promptly returned to the ant hill and was again picked up and taken to the burial spot. This time, when he returned to the ant hill, he was ignored. The pheromone odor had disappeared. Ants use pheromones to leave a trail of scent when returning from a food source to their hill. Other ants in the hill are attracted by the odor and follow the trail back to the food source. Pheromones lose their potency after a short time, so the trail to an exhausted food source disappears; more generally the air is cleared so that new chemical information can appear and not be confused with old information.

SIGNAL INTENSITY

It has been shown in the green heron and the rhesus monkey that the stronger the aggressive display, the more probable that the opponent will retreat. Three stages of increasing aggressiveness for the rhesus monkey and the green heron are shown in Figure 2.1. This increase in signal intensity seems analogous to human behavior. The misbehaving child may sense how likely it is that an irate parent is going to resort to spanking by the loudness of the parent's scolding. The child has become conditioned to loudness of voice as an indicator of how angry the parent is.[2] Some people may get quieter as they get angrier, but this occurs only when the expression of anger is under voluntary control. In animals the strength of the aggressive display depends only on the intensity of the sign stimulus and the consequent state aroused in

FIGURE 2.1. Stages of aggressive display in the rhesus monkey and green heron. (Redrawn from "Animal Communication," E.O. Wilson. Copyright © 1972 by Scientific American, Inc. All rights reserved.)

[2]*Conditioning.* Conditioning is a process of learning in which what is learned is the connection between a signal and pleasant or unpleasant consequences, called positive and negative reinforcement. For the misbehaving child in the example, the negative reinforcement is a spanking. The signal that communicates the likelihood of a spanking is a certain degree of loudness of the parent's voice. It has been shown experimentally many times that if a negative reinforcement (in this case, the spanking) is paired a few times with the signal preceding the painful stimulus (the loudness of voice), human beings and other subjects will stop the behavior when they hear the signal, avoiding the unpleasant consequences.

the animal making the display. The likelihood of a flight response from a species member depends on the intensity of the display.

HOW MANY SIGNALS?

As the number of studies of animal species in the wild increases, there will undoubtedly be changes in the estimated number of signals different animal species possess. There may well be differences in the way signals are defined. For example, herons and rhesus monkeys each have three gradations of their aggressive displays. Shall we say that each species has an aggressive display with three gradations or that each species has three different aggressive displays? The decision will influence the number of signals the species is reported to have. However, the important differences between the signal systems of animals in the wild and human language do not rest on whether the animal species with the largest known number of signals has 36, as reported by Wilson (1972) for the rhesus monkey, or 343, the number of intermediate, graded calls of the chimpanzee, which P. Marler (1976), cited by Bonner (1980), has grouped into 13 categories of vocalizations.

In Chapter Three, the signaling behavior of vertebrate animals as experimental animals in contact with human beings will be examined, along with evidence that vertebrate animals' signaling repertoires can be vastly increased. The important differences, however, are that animal signals are innate, involuntary, and limited in number while human language use is learned, intentional, and comprised of an infinite number of messages. More will be said on this topic in the course of this book.

BIRDSONG

To conclude this chapter, I want to present material based on the discussion of J. T. Bonner (1980) concerning birdsong. Parasite birds—that is, birds that lay their eggs in the nest of some other species so that the chicks never hear their species song—inherit their entire song. The male's ability to sing the song and the female's to recognize and respond to it with copulatory behavior are both innate, and necessarily so for the species' survival. Some species, the white crowned sparrow for example, partially learn their song by imitating mature males. This has been shown by isolating newborn males at birth and finding that the song they sing is significantly simpler than that sung by birds raised by their parents. The biologically adaptive advantage of learning part of the song, instead of inheriting it all, is in being able to recognize individuals by their calls and thus to locate a family member.

African strikes, which live in dense tropical forests, are an example of duetting birds. Male and female duetting birds either sing their song in unison or alternate so perfectly that, heard from a distance, they sound like a single bird. It is assumed that duetting is adaptive behavior because it makes it possible for the birds to keep track of each other in the dense forest.

be the explanation preferred to intentional learning in instances in which conditioning will account for acquisition of a new response by a subject.

Pets

When our cat, Lucy, stands in front of the refrigerator and meows, I give her something to eat; when she stands in front of the front door and meows, I let her out. She has been conditioned to produce these behaviors—meowing in particular locations—because I have correctly responded, thereby providing positive reinforcement. This happened in the natural course of events. I did not set out to condition Lucy to emit these informative behaviors. It might be said on Lucy's behalf that she probably did not set out to condition me either, but I do respond correctly to her signals. I am not sure how I became conditioned. I did not notice it happening. As I think about it, I realize that I avoid negative reinforcement by letting her out when she meows at the front door; I avoid having to clean out the catbox, or clean up a worse mess. The positive reinforcement for feeding her after she meows at the refrigerator must come from fulfillment of a caregiving impulse. I do not know whether she has attempted to elicit other behaviors from me by vocalizing. If she has, I have not understood, and she has ceased trying.

In Chapter One, I distinguished between communicative behavior, which is intentional, and signaling, which is an involuntary response elicited by a stimulus such as a particular smell or seeing a predator. Where does the kind of conditioned signaling behavior that Lucy displays belong? Once again, it cannot be proved that the behavior is not intentional, but the explanation that assumes the least in the way of higher mental processes on Lucy's part says that conditioned signaling behavior is like innate, animal signals; it is unintentional and is the result of having become conditioned to an internal sensation through positive reinforcement. Lucy's meowing in front of the refrigerator is a conditioned response to the internal sensation of hunger, acquired because food has been given her, reliably, when she has meowed in front of the refrigerator.

It is more difficult for me to make the assumption that her meowing at the front door is nothing but a conditioned response. In my thinking, Lucy's wanting to go out is associated with her being housebroken, but Lucy also uses a catbox in the house. The signaling behavior of animals in the wild is a simple response behavior. The animal has only one possible response to a stimulus. The sparrow that gives the alarm cry also flies off, but these are parts of the same response. The sparrow does not fly away occasionally without giving the alarm cry, or give the cry and *not* fly away. However, Lucy sometimes meows at the front door and at other times uses the catbox. She has two possible responses to the sensation. Which response she makes could reflect conditioning to particular temperatures. Perhaps this is the case as I have noticed that she meows at the front door only in the warm months of the year and does not step out of house between the end of October and the beginning of May.

Maybe I am wrong about the internal sensation that elicits Lucy's meowing at the front door. All I know is that she meows at the front door, and I let her out. If I were to watch her each time she goes out to see what she does, I would be able to check the hypothesis that her meowing to get out is a response to her being housebroken. I have not watched, so what I have is a plausible but unconfirmed hypothesis. Lucy's meow at the door could be the response to various internal sensations, such as a sexual urge or the urge to hunt. Both of these urges can be satisfied outdoors but not in the house. In order to settle the question in a way that would be entirely satisfactory to the empirical scientist, I would have to observe Lucy's behavior after she gets out of the house a sufficient number of times to see what her habitual patterns of behavior are. But finding that Lucy's meowing at the door is her response to several different internal sensations rather than just one would still leave unresolved the question of the intentionality of her meow at the door. Her behavior is consistent with both the explanation that it is conditioned and that it is intentional. The conditioning explanation makes less of an assumption of higher mental processes on Lucy's part, therefore, I will stand by the conditioning explanation.

The question of intentionality versus conditioning as the explanation for a behavior is important because intentionality is a defining characteristic of human language use. One claim that fond pet owners frequently make is that their pets understand what they say. I have an English friend who says to her dog, "Die for the Queen," whereupon the dog rolls over on its back with its feet in the air, the appropriate response. This anecdote is useful in helping people to take an objective view of pets' understanding of language. Few would claim that my friend's dog hears the sentence, "Die for the Queen," figures out what it implies for his behavior, and acts accordingly. Once the question is raised as to what the dog is responding to and how he learned his response, it can be seen that the utterance has signal properties to which the dog responds. The utterance has to have a particular sound pattern; "Die for the Queen?" spoken as a question will not evoke the rolling over response. Say "Die for the Queen" first as a command, then as a question, and note the different pitch patterns. For the command, pitch falls at the end of the utterance. For the question, pitch rises. Pitch pattern is one of the variables distinguishing different signals that trainers use with animals. Another is the length of the signal. "Heel!" and "Die for the Queen!" differ in length. Another very important part of the signal is the trainer's accompanying gesture or bodily movement. Animals probably do respond to actual word differences—dogs can differentiate "Down" from "Heel." However, the difference in the trainer's accompanying gesture may be more significant than the sound difference.

Experimental Animals

When human beings interact with experimental animals, the situation is like the interaction of trainers and pets. The human experimenter aims to teach the experimental animal(s). Over the years there has been controversy among animal behavior research psychologists about what animals have learned in animal learning experiments. Here again, the behavioral scientist will abide by Lloyd Morgan's canon and interpret the animal's learning in a way that assumes the least intelligence necessary to account for the animal's behavior, as I did, for example, in interpreting the dog's response to "Die for the Queen."

Experimental psychologists have taught rats to run mazes, cats to open doors, and many other kinds of animals to produce many other kinds of behavior. Of special relevance to this book is the experimental work aimed at teaching language to apes.

Linguistic Apes: A First Look

Sarah, a chimpanzee, was Ann James Premack's and David Premack's subject in a language teaching experimental program, which began in 1966. They have published an account of the early years of the program (Premack and Premack 1972). They presented their work as "teaching Sarah to read and write with variously shaped and coloured pieces of plastic, each representing a word." Their purpose in carrying out their experimental program with Sarah was, like mine, to assess the continuities between animal and human language capabilities. In carrying out their program they exploited the chimpanzee's conceptual abilities. All vertebrates are capable of treating different stimulus objects as equivalent. Asking the reader to pick the spoons out of the silverware drawer would be an example of requesting that stimulus objects be treated as equivalent. In order to respond the reader would also need to be able to differentiate spoons from forks and knives. All vertebrates are capable of differentiation. Species differ in the range of these abilities, which is a biological given for a species. The capacity to form equivalence classes is a cognitive ability but not a linguistic ability, and it can be observed in animal species for which no linguistic claims have been made.

Fascinating findings concerning the capacities of pigeons to treat stimulus objects as equivalent are described by Herrnstein et al. (1976). Herrnstein and his fellow researchers were not interested in teaching pigeons to form equivalence classes; instead they wanted to find out how pigeons naturally, visually discriminate objects like trees from other objects that, from a distance, might be mistaken for trees. They wanted to investigate the kind of stimulus objects pigeons would respond to as trees and the stimulus objects that the experimenters thought might be equivalent to trees for pigeons but which the pigeons would differentiate from trees.

The experimental subjects in this research were 11 male pigeons who had been raised on the seventh floor of Harvard University's behavioral sciences building and had never been outdoors. The stimuli were color slides projected on the front wall of a standard pigeon chamber. The pigeon being tested was conditioned to peck at a key in the presence of positive stimuli (such as, a picture of a house with branches of two trees visible) and not to peck in the presence of negative stimuli (such as, a vine with many leaves climbing on a cement wall). (See Figure 3.1.) Three experiments were carried out; they concerned the pigeon's ability to differentiate pictures of trees from nontrees, naturally lying water from nonwater, and one particular person from others. (Typical pictures that were correctly classified as trees and nontrees are shown in Figure 3.1.)

Herrnstein's experiment is relevant to understanding the development of language because it shows the pigeon's striking ability to classify naturally occurring stimulus objects that are significant to its biological adaptation. This is a *cognitive* ability, totally separate from the use of language, although sometimes mistaken for a linguistic ability.

In addition to the cognitive abilities to treat objects as equivalent and to learn to differentiate objects, most primates have the ability to relate categories to each other and respond to the relationship between objects rather than the object itself. So they can be taught to order three stimulus objects by size, for example (Lenneberg 1967).

Sarah and the other linguistic apes have another capacity; they are able to associate a sound or meaningless token with a class of object. In human beings this becomes the ability to label or name. Because apes lack the vocal abilities of human beings and at the same time are extremely dextrous, all contemporary linguistic apes are being taught some kind of visual manipulatory, rather than auditory, system. The Premacks used colored, plastic tokens to stand for words. Their method of teaching was conditioning with positive reinforcement in the form of foods Sarah likes. For example, Sarah was first conditioned to pair objects that were alike. Two apples and a banana were placed in front of her and she was rewarded for moving the apples close to each other and away from the banana. Then she was conditioned to place a gold-colored plastic token with jagged edges between two apples and a red plastic token with smooth edges between an apple and a banana (see Figure 3.2). These responses were conditioned to other objects including corks and bottle tops, and keys and rubber bands. Following this, Sarah was conditioned to replace a purple token with a hole in it, lying *between two corks,* with the jagged-edged, gold-colored token. If the purple token with the hole was lying *between the cork and bottle top,* Sarah was conditioned to replace the purple token with the smooth-edged, red token. This is a straightforward conditioning procedure in which the Premacks used bananas, raisins, apples, and others of Sarah's preferred foods (including chocolate) as the positive reinforcement. The difficulty with the Premacks work was their interpretation of it. To them the jagged-edged, gold-colored token stood for the

FIGURE 3.1.
Tree and nontree slides.

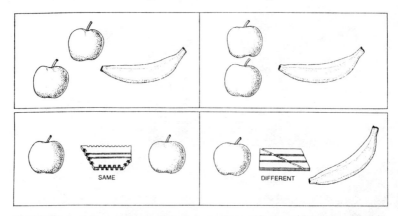

FIGURE 3.2. Tokens for conditioning studies with the chimpanzee Sarah. Gold-colored plastic token between two apples; red token, apple and banana. (From "Teaching Language to an Ape," Ann James Premack and David Premack. Copyright © 1972 by Scientific American, Inc. All rights reserved.)

word *same,* the smooth-edged, red token for the word *different,* and they wanted to impute the same linguistic status for the tokens to Sarah. They wanted to credit Sarah with understanding "apple same (as) apple" and "apple different (from) banana" in the presence of fruit and the tokens. It is not quite the same as imputing a linguistic interpretation of "Die for the Queen" to the dog who rolls over at the command. But it is still a matter of imputing a linguistic interpretation to behavior that is fully consistent with the interpretation that it is conditioned. It would not be possible to condition Sarah's behavior in this way if it were not for her innate capacity to see objects as equivalent (two apples) and different (an apple and banana). This is a cognitive capacity and, as we have seen, highly developed in the pigeon. It is not a linguistic capacity. In Chapter Seven, a human being, Genie, will be described who has cognitive abilities more than adequate to language development but has not been able to acquire a human language. Also in Chapter Seven, we will take another look at linguistic apes. As far as Sarah is concerned, and the Premacks have concurred, the information exchange with her using objects and plastic tokens is not language use, but the achievements of other linguistic apes, Washoe, Nim, and Koko remain to be described and evaluated.

4

The Prelinguistic Infant

The human infant is born with a repertoire of behaviors that are biologically adaptive for a being who will be completely dependent on the caregiving of others for survival. Newborn babies demonstrate sucking, grasping, clinging, and reaching responses, which underlie feeding and proximity-seeking and maintaining behavior. More immediately relevant to language development is the very young infant's signaling repertoire—the cries, cooing, smiling, and arm movements—that are effective in eliciting caregiving and affectionate responses from the mother or mother surrogate. Infant cries and arm movements are observed from shortly after birth. Smiling and cooing (comfort sounds) appear within a few weeks.

The newborn's repertoire of survival behaviors is adaptive, in just the way the innate repertoires of other animal species are, and is assumed to have developed because of its survival value in the human's environment. In the ecological niche occupied by the human species, language must be regarded as a biologically adaptive capacity. All human societies have language and no nonhuman species do. We want to consider how the cries, cooing, smiling, and arm movements of newborn infants support language development. Perhaps the best way to consider the transformation from these behaviors to language is to watch it happen.

THE INTERACTION OF INFANTS
WITH THEIR MOTHERS

My coworkers and I have watched the transformation by means of a research project called "How the human infant becomes a language user." We presented our project to parents of first-born infants whose mothers would be primary caretakers when the infants were about a month old. We described the project as an ethological, longitudinal study of infanthood. We said we would like to come every other week when the mother would ordinarily be undressing, bathing, dressing, and feeding the baby and videotape the mother and baby during this sequence. We have made such a series of tapes for two girl and two boy babies (Jean, Carol, Allen, and Joel) starting when each baby was ten weeks old, taping every other week until the babies were eighteen months old, and making a final tape when the babies were two years old. Because we always taped the same events, we can compare the behaviors of each mother-infant dyad (pair) at various times, observing changes over time, and we can also compare the dyads with each other. This makes it possible to see what is common in the infants' histories as they become language users and what is peculiar to particular infants.

The reader may wonder why we began taping the infants when they were so young, clearly many months before any would utter a single word. Our answer is that a great deal that is learned in becoming a language user is learned in the preverbal stage. During the preverbal period the human infant's innate signaling responses change, in part because of maturational changes in the infant. In addition the infant's vocalizations are influenced by verbal and vocal communications directed to the infant. We will look at these changes.

In describing developments during the preverbal stage that underlie human communicative behavior, we will consider separately phonological development (learning to produce speech sounds), the development of gestures, and of conversational competencies. The three kinds of developments are taking place simultaneously. What we and others (such as M. Richards, J. Newsome, J. Shotter, all in 1978) have found is that mothers behave toward their infants as though the infants' arm and body movements and babbles, cries, and vegetative noises were intended by the infants to be meaningful and to communicate meaning. At three months Joel is lying on the kitchen counter while his mother puts water in the sink to bathe him. Joel is waving his arms, and his left hand touches the wall near a flower on the wallpaper. His mother says, "Oh, you want the flower."

Human infants are like other baby animals in having innate signals that are informative. As we pointed out in Chapter Two, the signals are informative but they are not intentional. None the less, mothers treat babies' acts and vocalizations as intentional, and as the babies become mature enough to absorb the information, they can learn from their mothers' responses what their particular acts and vocalizations are taken to mean. Joel can learn that if you extend your arm in the direction of an object, it is taken to mean that you want the object to be handed to you. Calling replaces part of the infant's crying behavior as he becomes mature enough to *intend* to gain proximity to or care from the mother. Bowlby (1969) puts the development of calling sometime during the second year. The fact that caretakers have responded to the baby's reflexive crying provides the experience that makes learning to call possible.

A RECIPROCAL, INSTINCTUAL MODEL OF LANGUAGE DEVELOPMENT

Developmental psycholinguists (people who work on the development of human language and the differences between human language and animal signal systems) would agree that human beings have an innate predisposition to develop language; but language development does not happen without exposure to language, and the language developed is the one to which the infant-child is exposed. In researching how the human infant becomes a language user, I have found evidence that leads me to propose that, not only is the human infant innately predisposed to acquire language, but competent speakers (and perhaps mothers especially) are innately predisposed to use language in talking to very young children so as to *teach* them to use language (Holzman, 1983, unpublished). It looks as though the behavior of the baby that is fostering his language development elicits language behavior from the mother that is appropriate to the stage of development of the infant's language skills. It also appears that mothers' linguistic behavior provides feedback that elicits responses from infants that help them gain linguistic competence. In the course of Chapters Four, Five, and Seven, which discuss the prelinguistic, one-word, and after-the-one-word stages in language development, I describe the way language develops and present evidence from my research consistent with a reciprocal, instinctual model of language development. In Chapter Eight I will describe some research that suggests that linguistic behavior appropriate to the immature language user's stage of development is elicited from four-year-old, competent speakers.

LEARNING TO TAKE A CONVERSATIONAL TURN

We observed, beginning with our earliest videotapes, the mothers' imposition of a *conversational pattern* on the infants' vocalizations. The mother does this by fitting her verbalizations and/or vocalizations in between those of her baby and constructing them so that they imply that her baby's vocalizations, vegetative noises (burps, wheezes, and so on), and actions were intended as contributions to the conversation. C. Snow (1977), and C. Trevarthen and G. Hubley (1978) have reported a similar finding. The effect of the mother's behavior is to provide the circumstances in which her infant can learn the first rules for participating in a conversation: only one person speaks at a time and both get a turn. Here is a turntaking sequence with Carol and her mother when Carol was three months and four days old. Carol had been nursing; she stopped and looked into her mother's eyes. Mother is holding Carol's hand:

Carol	*Mother*

1. [ɛ̄] (This has the sound of the *e* in *bed.* The flat line over the **ɛ** means that the pitch did not rise or fall.)
2. [ʌ̀] (The sound is that of *u* in *but.* The slanted line indicates falling pitch.)

                                                      3. what

4. [ɑ̂] (*a* is the sound of *o* in *bother.*)

                                                      5. yeah

6. [aw aw] (is the sound of *w* in *witch.*)

                                                      7. really

8. [ʌwaw] (*w* is the sound of *w* in *witch.*)

                                                      9. okay

10. [ah ah ah] (*h* is the sound in *hat.*)
11. burp

                                                     12. fantastic

Carol's vocalizations have been transcribed from the videotape in the notation of the International Phonetic Alphabet.[1] If speech or vocalizations are transcribed using the IPA, then anyone who knows this system can read the transcription and figure out how the speech or vocalization sounded. IPA is used by linguists and anthropologists to communicate unambiguously about how speech samples sound. Speech in any language, as well as babble like Carol's, can be transcribed using the IPA. The portion of the IPA relevant to the English transcription is reproduced in Chapter Seven. The square brackets surrounding Carol's vocalizations indicate that the transcription is phonetic, made on the basis of the sounds in Carol's vocalizations. When a transcription is enclosed by two slanted lines (//) rather than square brackets, the vocalization is a speech sound (including words and sentences) in the language being transcribed. This is called a *phonemic* transcription and can be made only if the transcriber knows which sounds being produced are phonomes, or meaning-relevant speech sounds. Since Carol does not yet have language, her vocalizations are not phonemic. The speaker must intend to be speaking words, and the transcriber must understand which words the speaker is saying for a phonemic transcription to be made. The transcriptions would still be made in the phonetic symbols of the IPA, but with the slanted line brackets meaning these speech sounds are phonemes of the English language. Carol's mother's utterances have been transcribed *orthographically* (in the written English alphabet).

The lines above Carol's and her mother's utterances give the pitch contours of their utterances. We pay attention only to whether pitch is rising, falling, or steady and not to how much or how fast pitch rise and falls.

---

[1]The notation used in this book is in the American tradition. There is some variation in symbols used by people in various countries of the world.

I have said that babies utter noncry vocalizations from the first day of life, but the young infant's repertoire of sounds is quite limited. For the most part, the sounds are produced when the baby opens its mouth, and lets air out with no oral obstruction and with enough tension on the vocal cords to cause them to vibrate and produce sound. The vocalization is not intended to have a particular sound like *dog* or *car.* Babies have to learn how to move their lips and tongues to make intentional sounds. Consonant-vowel combinations are produced inadvertently from time to time when the baby's mouth is closed and the mother shifts its weight so that air is pushed out of the vocal tract. If the baby's mouth is closed, the air is obstructed and a consonant sound, [b] for example, produced as the air is expelled through the baby's mouth. For the most part young babies do not produce high vowels—the vowel *sounds* in *sea, bit, poor, foot,* for example. In the early months the baby does not intend to produce a particular sound. If a vocalization sounds like *ma,* it is because *ma* does not require any elaborate movements in the baby's vocal apparatus. As the baby matures, he gains increasing control over his breathing and vocal apparatus and is able to produce a wide range of vowel sounds and vowel-consonant combinations.

The first evidence from the language development research involving Allen, Carol, Jean, and Joel for a reciprocal, instinctual model came from Goldner's findings (1981) on turntaking between the infants and their mothers. In the course of her work on my research project Goldner transcribed all the turntaking episodes on the tapes made nearest to the dates when the infants were 3, 6, 9, 12, 15, 18, and 24 months old. Goldner observed that the number of each mother's verbalizations over the two years that included nonsensical vocalization increased to a peak percentage and then steadily declined (see Figure 4.1). The three month (p. 26) and nine month (p. 28) interaction episodes presented for Carol and her mother show the change in mother behavior. Vocalizing by the mother is a retrograde (moving backward) linguistic behavior, and yet increases, in combination with verbalization, in the baby's first nine months to a year of life.

How would increased babbling by the mother foster language acquisition by her infant? The obvious possibility is that it fosters the infant's gaining control over his vocal tract and respiratory system so that he becomes able to intentionally produce speech sounds. Two teaching procedures can be observed in the mother's behavior: modeling and shaping. Modeling simply means producing a particular sound so the infant can hear it and perhaps attempt it. Shaping is a procedure in which an infant vocalization is gradually altered by providing a model that changes by successive approximations to the desired behavior. The infant emits a babble and the mother responds with a babble, sometimes an imitation of the infant's, but a sound that is phonologically closer to English than the infant's babble. It is not that the mother necessarily intends to shape the infant's vocalizations. Because she is an English speaker, she cannot help giving her babbles the phonological characteristics of English. Here is an interaction between Carol

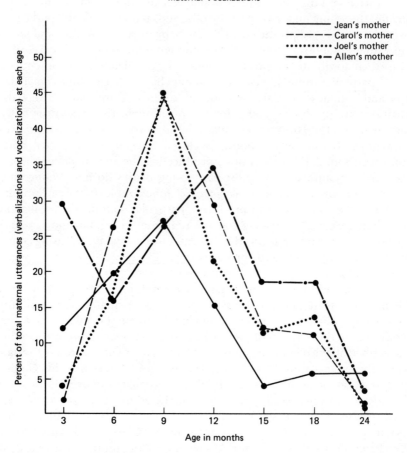

Maternal Vocalizations

FIGURE 4.1. Mother vocalizations as a percent of vocalizations plus verbalizations. (From Goldner, 1981)

and her mother when Carol was nine months old. Carol is in the bath tub being washed by mother.

Carol

1. [aw] chews on washcloth

3. [m̂]
4. [m̄]
5. [hwh waɛ yɛh]

8. [ʔɛ m]

10. [hya͡ hya͡ hya͡]

Mother

2. It's nice, huh?

6. [hɛʌɛ] [hm hm]
7. [hm hm]
9. [ʔoh]

11. [hya͡ hya͡ hya͡]

28

If you look back at the interaction between Carol and her mother at three months, you will see the mother's shift from verbal to vocal.

LEARNING TO USE
THE PITCH CONTOURS
AND THE SOUNDS OF SPEECH

Mothers probably are not consciously aware of responding more frequently to babies' vocalizations with vocalizations of their own rather than verbalizations. Unconsciously they are led to vocalize because their babies evidence greater interest in their vocalizing, reflected in the infants' greater responsiveness to vocalizing. Mothers' vocalizing is positively reinforced by the infants' response to it. If we assume that it is biologically adaptive for human beings to have language, then we can suppose that the mothers' increased vocalizing serves a biological function—the infant's acquiring the phonology of language. If we listen to the cooing or babbling of very young infants, we cannot tell what language their native language will be. If we listen a year or so later, we can hear the intonation (pitch contours) and phonetic structure (speech sounds) of the language they hear.

We have examined samples of the babies' babbles and mothers' vocal responses during the infants' first year. The following examples are for Allen. We find some true imitations in which the mother accurately produces both the infant's pitch and phonological form as

1. Allen: [ʔah]   2. Mother: [ʔah]

Mothers also produce *stereotyped* baby noises in which the mother's response is not closely related to the infant's production. Processes of conventionalization appear to be at work. A mother will produce an "Anglicized" form of noises her baby is currently making. What often happens is that, after one or two close imitations, the mother slips into her stereotyped form, which may be produced in order to elicit more interaction by the baby.

Allen	Mother
2. [m̃]	1. [m̃]
	3. [m̃]
	4. [m̃]
5. [m̃]	

[m̃] is a stereotyped utterance produced by Allen in the second year, together with an open handed reach, a gestural-vocal communication indicating a desire to be given something out of his reach.

Here is another conventionalized response:

1. Allen: [əgʌ]   2. Mother: [gu]

In our culture babies are supposed to say "goo"; so, when Allen said "[əgʌ]" his mother's imitation moved the vocalization in the direction of the cultural stereotype for baby talk.

At 12 months and increasingly at 15 and 18 months, mothers imitate the pitch contour on a baby vocalization but produce an English word closely related phonetically to the baby's production.

1. Allen: [ɛ̂]   2. Mother: yeah
1. Carol: [bo]   2. Mother: boat, boat
1. Joel: [NæNæ]   2. Mother: No

We can interpret Figure 4.1 in this way: mother vocalizations to her baby increase during the first months of the infant's life because the baby becomes more responsive to vocalizations in comparison to verbalizations. The mother's increased vocalizations are imitations of the infant's vocalizations, but include other vocalizations that are phonologically like English. It appears that this moves the infant's vocalizations in the direction of English phonology. Beginning at 12 months for three of the babies and 15 months for the fourth, mother vocalizations decline. Mothers are still responding imitatively to baby vocalizations—but selectively. If a baby vocalization resembles an English word, the mother utters the word.

Here are examples of Carol's and Joel's interaction with their mothers at 18 months:

Carol's mother puts Carol in the bath tub and says

Carol	*Mother*
	1. Hot today.
2. [ko]	
	3. Cold

Carol points to the camera person and says

1. Carol: [t s ah]   2. Mother: Joanne, right.

Joel is sitting in the bath tub; he smiles at his mother, grinds his teeth, and says

1. Joel: [t ih]   2. Mother: teeth

A little later, Joel is just sitting in the tub, mother catches his eye and whispers

Joel	*Mother*
	1. No (whispered)
2. laughs	
	3. No (whispered but louder)

4. $\overparen{[dɛh]}$

6. $\overparen{[dɛh]}$

8. laughs

5. Y̆es (normal voice)

7. Y̆es (normal voice)

Mothers continue to vocalize nonimitatively to their babies but at low rates and in ways similar to the early months. Carol's mother says, "D$\overparen{ubba}$, d$\overparen{ubba}$, d$\overparen{ubba}$" as she dries Carol at 15 months. Vocalizing has ceased having a teaching function for these mothers.

We started this discussion by pointing out that, before babies are verbal, they can learn the two basic rules of conversation: one person at a time and both get turns. In the course of the discussion we have seen that, in this small sample, mothers are (probably unconsciously) teaching their infants how to make babbles sound like English words and conversations, and the infants are learning English phonology. In the examples presented for Carol and Joel and their mothers at 18 months, we would be tempted to say Carol and Joel really know these words but cannot pronounce them. I think this is the case.

LEARNING TO PARTICIPATE IN A RITUALIZED GAME

Even though the baby becomes a partner in turntaking episodes with his mother (rather than simply having her fit her contributions around his so that a turntaking pattern results), some of these episodes remain simply rituals. In many instances, including the games infants are taught to play, this is true. We have watched infants learning to participate in games like Peekaboo. The earliest instance we have seen involved an infant, Sue, and her mother, whom we studied during Sue's first year.

When Sue was almost five months old, we first observed her mother, with Sue supine on the changing table and ready to be freshly diapered, throw a diaper over Sue's head and croon, "Where's the baby? Where's the baby?" She then removed the diaper and very brightly and enthusiastically called, "There's the baby!" Two weeks later, after her mother had carried out the routine through the two "where's the baby" utterances, Sue removed the diaper from her own face, and then her mother said, "There's the baby!" By the time Sue was six months old, Sue both covered her face with the diaper and removed it. In our observation at six months, the moment Sue's mother noticed Sue was pulling the diaper over her face, she quickly sang out, "Where's the baby, where's the baby?" Sue pulled the diaper away from her face, and her mother said, "There's the baby!" During our next observation the mother was somewhat preoccupied as she diapered Sue. Sue pulled the diaper on and off her face with no response from her mother, who was jabbering about "baa, baa, black sheep." Again Sue pulled the diaper on and off her face with still no response from her mother, so this time Sue provided an elongated vocalization herself after pulling the diaper off her face. Even though Sue "knows" that "where's the baby" has a sequence (face covered, vocalization with rising pitch, face uncovered, vocalizations with level or falling pitch), she doesn't know what the actions or the vocalizations mean or signify. It's a little routine she has learned to do with her mother. Usually her mother is very interested in the game; her mother smiles, talks in a loving voice, and displays behaviors that are reinforcing to Sue at an age when she has strong attachment needs. So, going through the ritual is rewarding to Sue, even though she does not understand the question, "Where's the baby?" or that pulling the diaper away from her face provides the appropriate occasion for the response, "There's the baby." It is sound and action play, and the sounds do not have the meaning of words in the English language. Preverbal infants' linguistic abilities are just like those of the pets described in the last chapter. The fact that my friend's dog rolls over on its back with its feet up in the air when my friend says, "Die for the Queen!" doesn't mean the dog understands the meaning of "Die for the Queen" in the English language. It is a sound signal to which the dog has been conditioned to give the appropriate behavior; such is the case with the prelinguistic, or preverbal, infant.

GESTURES INTO WORDS

Infants are at the beginning of a developmental sequence that will culminate in their becoming language users. Therefore their rituals and gestures, which are borderline linguistic behaviors, have significance because they are not part of the infants' repertoire of innate signaling behaviors but have been acquired in interaction with their mothers. We distinguish between rituals (including games like Peekaboo) and imitations on the one hand and gestures on the other on the basis of the function of the behaviors for the person engaging in them. Gestures have an instrumental function; rituals and imitation have a social play or practice function. The clearest example of a gesture by the infants we have observed is the requesting or directive gesture. It has also been observed in infants by A. Carter (1978), L. Menn (1976), and E. Bates (1976) among others. It consists of an open-handed reach accompanied by a vocalization with rising pitch contour. For Allen the vocalization we observed was [M̃m]; for Carol, [z̄ī s]; for Jean, [ãh]; and for Joel, [dãɛ]. Since we observed for only a half hour every other week, it is quite possible that the babies used requesting gestures other than the ones we observed.

The evolution of the gesture is first from innate arm extending movement to visually directed behavior. Not all reaches culminate in the infant's securing the object for which he is reaching. When an infant reaches unsuccessfully and at the same time vocalizes in the presence of his mother in an attention-attracting manner so that the mother (1) looks at her infant, (2) looks in the direction of his reach, and (3) offers him or points to a possible object and says, for example, "Do you want this?" circumstances are right for the gestures to be learned. It is learned by conditioning as are the animals' learned signs described in Chapter Three. The instrumental function of the requesting or directive behavior is to get someone to do something for you by indicating that you want it done. If the mother offers her infant what the infant wants, the requesting behavior is positively reinforced and is learned so that the infant will use that gesture appropriately. We have discussed the fact that infant vocalizations are moved in the direction of English words in their mothers' responses to them, and sometimes there is good evidence that vocalizations are the infant's intended approximations of English words. In the early stage when infants become capable of using a vocalization with rising pitch together with an open-handed reach to produce a requesting gesture, it is not of much significance whether the vocalization is a word or just a consistent sound. Whichever it is, it has no meaning for the infant except as part of his requesting gesture. We will consider this the borderline period between prelinguistic and linguistic periods in the development of language.

Carol accompanied her reach with the vocalizations [zĪs]. It looks as though [zĪs] is Carol's reproduction of the last word in her mother's question, "Do you want this?" Allen used [m̄m] and Jean [āh] in the same way that Carol used [zĪs], but we were not tempted to call these words because they do not sound like words.

It is plausible that Joel's [d æ] is his rendering of *that,* analogous to Carol's rendering of *this.* We do not have evidence from the videotape that this is the case for Joel; Joel's mother has not asked Joel if he wants *that*—at least not on the videotapes. But Joel has used [d æ] three times in his request gestures, and never another word or vocalization, so the criteria described in Chapter Five for status as a word are met by [dæ]. We have put the beginning of the linguistic period earlier than some theorists would. These theorists would date the beginning of the linguistic period when the child uses words for *reference,* to name an object to which the child is calling attention.

WORDS IN RITUALS

One reason for deciding to date the linguistic period from the first three occurrences of the first word is that it is sometimes difficult to judge whether a child is actually naming an object as opposed to participating in a little ritual.

We have an example of Joel's imitating the word *kitty,* combined with a pointing gesture, at 12 months. Joel's mother had, since Joel was ten months old, engaged in pointing at objects and naming them for Joel. To a child who has not cracked the sound-meaning code, pointing plus uttering a word is learned as a ritual.

Here is an example of an exchange between Joel and his mother in their backyard:

Joel: (points to a bear in picture book) [k̄i k̄i]
Mother: That's not a kitty. That's a bear.
Joel: (points to kitty in book.) [k̄i]
Mother: Kitty. Uh huh. Gee that kitty just comes out all over the place.
Joel: (points to grasshopper).
Mother: That's a grasshopper. He's drinking from the kitty's water.
Joel: [k̄i] (points to boat)
Mother: Kitty, there's a kitty. (points to kitty)
Joel: [k̄i] (points to kitty)
Mother: Kitty. Uh huh.
Joel: (takes blocks with pictures out of toy box, points to kitty on a block)
Mother: Where's the kitty cat? There's the kitty cat. That's right. Where's the kitty cat again? Where's the kitty cat?
Joel: (points to chicken)
Mother: That's a chicken. Where's the kitty cat?
Joel: (points to bunny)
Mother: Bunny. That's a bunny. Where's the kitty cat? Show me the kitty cat?
Joel: (points to snail) [k̄i]
Mother: Kitty? That's not a kitty. That's a snail.

Joel has learned the word combined with a pointing gesture as an imitation of his mother. He has the word plus gesture as a social ritual, and again by the criteria described in Chapter Five, [ki] is counted as a word.

At this point these infants are making the transition to language use; they are learning to articulate the sounds of their language and to enjoy imitative rituals involving words. Further, they have learned to use rising pitch in their request vocalizations. This can be added to the two conversational rules—one at a time and each gets a turn. Rising intonation (pitch contour) on the end of an utterance indicates that there is more to come; the discourse has not been concluded. In a conversation, if a speaker ends an utterance with rising intonation, this indicates that the speaker wants to pass the turn to another participant. In the case of the infant's request gesture, the turn is being passed to the mother to fulfill the baby's request. The prelinguistic period comes gradually to an end as the infant begins to incorporate an approximation of an English word into request gestures and/or the social games and rituals. The infant learns first words in a social interaction with another human being, and the infant learns, as part of learning the word, the appropriate intonation for the word in that kind of social interaction. In other words, the infant is not learning the word; rather, the infant is learning to *use* the word in a particular social interaction.

5

The One-Word Period

In Chapter Four, we looked at developments in the prelinguistic infant's behavior related to the infant's becoming a language user. We noted that infants learned the first rules for participating in a conversation: one at a time, both get a turn. They learned to imitate, or learn by rote, what to them were just sounds but are actually English words. They also learned to employ what started out as an instrumental act as a gesture. That is, they all acquired a request or directive gesture based on reaching for an object (the instrumental act) and, at the same time, making a noise to get their mothers' attention. In this chapter we will consider the shift from action to discourse in carrying out interpersonal functions and the evolution of sounds and gestures into words. These developments take place in the course of the infant language learner's daily life, and for Allen, Carol, Jean, and Joel, it was primarily in interaction with their mothers. These infants became language users, as do most human beings, as part of their normal experience. Our understanding of the process has been greatly enhanced by conceptualizing verbalizations as speech acts as well as *linguistic* entities, such as sentences, nouns, verbs, adjectives, and so on.[1]

SPEECH ACTS

The idea of speech acts goes back to the work of the English philosopher of language, J. L. Austin. In his book *How to Do Things with Words* (1962), he examines the differences between *statements* like

---

[1] Human language as linguistic systems will be considered at length in Chapter Six. In this chapter I will mention and explain only as much as is necessary to talk about the one-word period.

1. I've been faithful all my life.
2. There is a cow in the yard.

and performatives like:

3. I promise that I will serve you faithfully all my life.
4. I sentence you to ten years in prison, (said by the judge to the prisoner standing before him in court at the conclusion of the trial).

The statements are reports about phenomena that the person making the statement is communicating. Statements always express a proposition. In the two examples; "I have been faithful all my life," and "There is a cow in the yard," the propositional content is all there is to the statements. Propositions specify an idea, person, or object, for example, and make a comment about it. In (1), *I* is the person specified or referred to, and *have been faithful all my life* is the comment the proposition makes or the *predicating expression.* In (2), *a cow* is the object specified, and *is in the yard* is the comment or predicating expression. Performatives are acts that are accomplished simply by saying the words in the appropriate circumstances (that is, one cannot pass sentence unless one is a judge who has just tried a suspect). Performatives do not express propositions. "I promise that I will serve you faithfully" makes a promise to the person addressed, and "I sentence you to ten years" sentences the person addressed to prison. Austin was interested in the fact that propositions can be analyzed to determine whether they are true or false while performatives cannot be so analyzed. Instead there are *conditions* that must be met for them to be successfully carried out. There are *appropriateness* conditions, such as being a judge addressing a suspect, and *sincerity* conditions, which means that a promise must be sincere or it is not a promise. But there is no way to talk meaningfully about true and false sentencing to prison or promising to serve. If the person passing sentence is not a judge in a court addressing the prisoner, the appropriateness condition for the speech act is not met. If a person is lying when making a promise, the sincerity condition for carrying out the speech act is not met. The various speech acts have sets of conditions that must be met for the successful carrying out of the speech act.

The idea of the speech act was developed and made more directly relevant to the study of language development during the 1960s by J. R. Searle, another philosopher of language. Searle (1969) conceptualized speaking a language as "performing speech acts—acts such as making statements, giving commands, asking questions, making promises and so on." Speech acts are understood by the hearer because they are performed in accordance with the rules that govern their success, and these rules are learned along with the other aspects of language use. Searle saw that it was not necessary to all speech acts that they contain a performative verb. The legal speech acts, "I *sentence* you to jail," "I *pronounce* you husband and wife," require the performative verb. But the speech act of warning, for example, does not.

5. I'll break your neck if you don't pay me back my money.
6. I warn you that I will break your neck if you don't pay me back my money.

That is, (5) is just as much a warning as (6), though it lacks the performative verb *I warn.*

This insight led to Searle's analyzing language use as performance of speech acts with two principal components—what he referred to as illocutionary force and propositional content. For purposes of my research in language development, I have found that distinguishing utterer's meaning or function of the speech act from its syntactic-semantic meaning, its meaning in the (English) language, makes it possible to conceptualize the continuity between animal signal systems and human language in a clear way. Recall, I said that my friend's dog responded to utterer's meaning (roll over) when my friend said "Die for the Queen" without understanding "Die for the Queen" as an English sentence. The distinction between utterer's meaning and syntactic-semantic meaning of the sentence in the English language roughly corresponds to Searle's illocutionary force and propositional content. Utterer's meaning is exactly the same as illocutionary force. Propositional content is related to syntactic-semantic meaning but is not identical to it. It is not worthwhile in this book to analyze the relationship further.

The Primitive Speech Act

In work on human language development, the most widely held idea concerning the status of one-word utterances of infants was, until the 1970s, that the one-word utterance stood for a sentence. This led to calling one-word utterances *holophrases,* meaning one-word sentences. John Dore (1975) proposed that the one-word utterances of infants should be conceptualized not as holophrases but as primitive speech acts. Dore pointed out that this avoided the problems of trying to figure out what the sentence might be that the holophrase represented but still took account of the intonational and gestural components of the one-word communication. This was important because it was the contrasts in the intonational and the gestural accompaniments of one-word utterances that had encouraged the idea that one-word utterances mean more than the meaning of the single word. Dore saw that the single words were being used to carry out different functions and that contrasting intonation and gestures distinguished functions. For example, the infant, Dory, points to her mother's necklace and says "/bidz/," labeling or referring to the necklace. Later, after Dory has been allowed to play with the necklace and her mother takes it back, Dory says "/bidz/," requesting that the necklace be returned to her.

We have discussed the learning by Allen, Carol, Jean, and Joel to put final rising intonation on a vocalization or word while making a reaching gesture in order to ask for something, thereby performing what Dore termed a primitive speech act. Dore called the rising intonation plus reach the primitive force of the speech act. The word that the infant speaks (with the rising intonation) is the rudimentary referring expression, or all the language there is in the primitive speech act. One-word requests like Carol's /zĪs/, can be interpreted only by looking at what Carol seems to be reaching for and checking with Carol. This is what her mother did. When Allen reached for his turtle-shaped bar of soap and said "/tŪrtl/," he was using a primitive referring expression to ask for the soap.

It seems plausible that the requesting speech act developed initially from a failure on the infant's part to reach a desired object. The infant continued holding out its hand, which didn't reach, in the direction of the object and made a vocal noise which attracted its mother's attention. She looked in the direction of the reach, offered the object the infant seemed to want, and maybe a second or third if the first wasn't satisfactory. If the routine was successful, the infant's vocalization plus reach, the primitive speech act, could be conditioned in just the way behaviors of pets and experimental animals have been. Securing the desired but unreachable object would provide the positive reinforcement to condition the reach plus vocalization.

I regard the primitive speech acts as continuous with the signaling behavior of animals in contact with people, described in Chapter Three. Distinguishing utterer's meaning and meaning of the sentence in the language makes it possible to analyze the function of the speech act separately from its formal characteristics as an expression in the English language.[2]

There would be no point in applying such an analysis to the signaling behavior of animals in the wild because each signal has a single function, that is, each signal conveys particular information; the sending of the information is involuntary and its effect on the animals who receive it is involuntary. All is the result of innate coordinations that were biologically adaptive in the animals' environment of biological adaptation. The situation is different when we consider animals in contact with human beings and infants. Both become conditioned to respond to and to produce learned signaling behavior.[3]

There are differences of opinion regarding the relationship of the function of a speech act (what the speaker meant by the utterance) and the formal properties of the utterance as a sentence in the English language. Searle (1969) proposed that the relationship is quite direct, that the formal characteristics determine what function can be expressed. In my research

---

[2]Speech acts are performed using any language. I say English language because that is the language of Allen, Carol, Jean, and Joel.

[3]Certain parts of some bird songs are not innate but learned from hearing the full song after a bird is born.

(Holzman 1972, 1974), I have found many instances in which the speaker was using an utterance in a way that was quite indirectly related to formal characteristics of the utterance. As we have seen, it is possible for pets and trained animals to understand what their trainer means by an utterance without any understanding of the utterance as a sentence in the English language. I think the same is true of infants; they understand what their mothers mean by an utterance before they understand the utterance as a sentence in the English language. And they understand on the same basis that they are understood, by means of the intonation and gestures that go along with utterances. Mothers' speech to their infants is characterized by short and frequently repeated utterances that focus on the here and now so that what is happening to the infant is glossed over and over in the mother's speech in utterances short enough to have clear signal value. I feel reasonably confident that this is the case, not only on the basis of my own work, but also because there is general agreement among child language specialists that infants respond to *prosodic* features of utterances (stress and pitch patterns) before they understand actual words or sentences. This is not unlike the response of pets.

All through the one-word period, the infant's speech acts remain primitive speeh acts because utterances are limited to one word. However, in this period word meanings evolve so that by the end of the one-word period, they have become abstract (whereas, at the beginning of the period, a word had only ritual, gestural, or occasion meaning—meanings which tied a word to a particular function or speech act).

STAGES IN THE ONE-WORD PERIOD

The beginning of the one-word period is tricky to pinpoint because of difficulties in deciding when an utterance is actually a word. Sometimes what sounds like a word is simply a vocalization whose sound, by chance, resembles that of an English word. In the research on the development of language by Allen, Carol, Jean, and Joel, we have a rule that infant vocalizations are not counted as words until they occur on the videotapes three separate times. This prevents our counting as words the vocalizations that accidentally sound like words. Further, we note from the videotape what the word means or how it is used. There has to be consistency of meaning or of occasion for use in the three occurrences as well as consistency of sound for the vocalization to count as a word. We included as words imitations by the child of its mother, words that occurred as parts of rituals, and words used gesturally as described in Chapter Four. In these cases, the words do not have referential meaning—that is, words are not being used by the infant to refer to objects or other aspects of his world; rather, they are used on occasions that have become associated for the child with a particular verbal behavior on the child's part. The game of Peekaboo, widely played by infants and caregivers, provides the occasion for the one who has been hiding his or her face to show it and for the other to say *peekaboo. Hello, goodbye,* and other greetings are also verbalizations that have occasion meaning rather than referential meaning. Parents usually understand that a child's word is a word when the child has a consistent meaning for it or occasion for its use, even if it does not sound the conventional way. Little children sometimes have difficulty pronouncing some speech sounds, and we make allowance for this. When Carol was saying [zIs], reaching for something out of reach, and looking at her mother (and this was the *only* circumstances in which she used [zIs]) [zIs] was a signal or gesture rather than an abstract word. When Joel went through the ritual with his mother of pointing at a picture, a bug, or an animal and saying [ki], (described in Chapter Four) and this was his only use of [ki], the use was not referential. The occasion I feel least comfortable calling word use is imitation, the most primitive speech act. The child imitates a word his mother has said. It may not even be a word from the sentence she has just said but may be from a sentence said several sentences before.

The one-word period as we have defined it has an early stage (A) in which words are used in only one way as explained above, a more advanced stage (B) when the word is used in carrying out more than one speech act, and a final stage (C) when the child has experienced the nominal insight (Dore 1978) that everything has a name.

Little children are not able to think about their thoughts and beliefs, so it is impossible to get meaningful answers from them to questions such as, "Do you remember before you could really talk what you thought when your mother said, 'Where's the baby?,' or you said, 'kitty' and pointed at a grasshopper or 'this' and held out your hand for your duck?" One source of information about preverbal memories is Helen Keller's autobiography, *The Story of My Life.* Helen Keller was almost seven years old when Annie Sullivan came to Helen's home in Alabama to teach her. In Helen Keller's book events are recounted by Helen and, in addition, are reported in extracts from the letters of Annie Sullivan to Mrs. Sophia C. Hopkins, who had been a matron at Perkins Institution and "like a mother" to Annie Sullivan when she had been a pupil there. The book is fascinating as a human document. In addition, the early chapters are relevant to the question of what it is like to be without language. It must be remembered that Helen Keller was also without sight and hearing so that her experience of the world came from touch, taste, and smell only. She was cut off from the world in a way that infants are not. Despite her terrible disabilities she was, according to Annie Sullivan, a large, strong, and ruddy child "as unrestricted in her movement as a young colt. She has none of these nervous habits that are so noticeable and so distressing in blind children." (Helen Keller, *The Story of My Life.* [Reprint, New York: Dell, 1978], p. 260.)

What I found surprising is that she had a substantial repertoire of gestures that she used to communicate with her family and others before

Annie Sullivan came. For example, she played with a little girl, Martha Washington, the child of the Kellers' cook. Helen tells how she liked to hunt for guinea fowl eggs, found in the long grass of out-of-the-way places. "I could not tell Martha Washington when I wanted to go egg hunting, but I would double my hands and put them on the ground, which meant something round in the grass, and Martha always understood" (ibid., p. 25). Helen had a large stock of such gestures, which, as she describes them, were like the early one-word-period gestures specific to one function of Allen, Carol, Jean, and Joel. When Annie Sullivan arrived at Helen Keller's home, she was met by Helen.

> [Helen] felt my face and dress and my bag, which she took out of my hand and tried to open. It did not open easily, and she felt carefully to see if there was a key hole. Finding that there was she turned to me making the sign of turning a key and pointing to the bag. Her mother interfered at this point and showed Helen by signs that she must not touch the bag (ibid., p. 259).

Helen considered her signs to be gestures rather than words. Even though they made it possible for Helen to communicate with family and friends and to be communicated with, Helen reports that her use of gestures never led to her gaining the understanding that "everything has a name."

The preverbal gestural repertoires of Allen, Carol, Jean, and Joel were much more limited than that of Helen Keller, but their gestures functioned in the same way as Helen's to get someone to do something. Helen Keller does not report having gestures that were just for social play purposes, which Allen, Carol, Jean, and Joel had. When Annie Sullivan first spelled *d-o-1-1* and other words into one of Helen's hands, at the same time giving Helen the doll or other object in her other hand, Helen learned to finger spell and associate spellings with objects without understanding that the spelling was the object's name. Helen Keller later wrote:

> The morning after my teacher came she gave me a doll—when I had played with it a little while, Miss Sullivan slowly spelled into my hand the word, "d-o-l-l." I was at once interested in this finger play and tried to imitate it. When I finally succeeded in making the letters correctly I was flushed with childish pride and pleasure. I did not know that I was spelling a word or even that words existed, I was simply making my fingers go in monkey-like imitation. In the days that followed I learned to spell in this incomprehending way a great many words, among them *pin, hat, cup,* and a few verbs like *sit, stand,* and *walk* (ibid., p. 33).

Helen Keller had a large repertoire of gestures that she understood and produced before Annie Sullivan came to teach her. But having words as names is very different. It depends on understanding that words have referential meaning. The understanding that words name objects came to Helen Keller in a dramatic moment.

> One day, while I was playing with my new doll, Miss Sullivan put my big rag doll in my lap also, spelled "d-o-l-l" and tried to get me to understand that "d-o-l-l"

applied to them both. Earlier in the day we had a tussle over the words "m-u-g" and "w-a-t-e-r." Miss Sullivan had tried to impress on me that "m-u-g" is *mug* and "w-a-t-e-r" is *water,* but I persisted in confounding the two. . . . She brought me my hat and I knew I was going out into the warm sunshine, and this thought, if a wordless sensation can be called a thought, made me hop and skip with pleasure. We walked down to the well house. . . . Someone was drawing water and my teacher placed my hand under the spout. As the cool stream gushed over one hand she spelled into the other hand, *water,* first slowly and then rapidly. I stood still, my whole attention fixed upon the motions of her fingers. Suddenly I felt a misty consciousness as of something forgotten—a thrill of returning thought; and somehow the mystery of language was revealed to me. I knew then that "w-a-t-e-r" meant the cool something that was flowing over my hand. That living word awakened my soul, gave it light, hope, joy, set it free! (ibid., p. 34)

Annie Sullivan described what happened next.

A new light came in to her face. She spelled *water* several times. Then she dropped on the ground and asked for *its* name and pointed to the pump and the trellis, and suddenly turning around she asked for my name. I spelled *teacher.* . . . All the way back to the house she was highly excited and learned the name of every object she touched so that in a few hours she had added 30 new words to her vocabularly (ibid., p. 274).

As far as I can tell from what Helen Keller and Annie Sullivan have written, Helen's gestures remained like the words of Allen, Carol, Jean, and Joel at the beginning of the one-word stage. Each gesture was used by Helen for just one function until she had the insight that "everything has a name." Helen did not experience the intermediate stage in which a word is used for more than one function but still does not have the abstract status of a name or what we, technically, call a common noun. I think the reason for this is that her blindness and deafness deprived her of the experiences that foster the development of occasion meaning for words. Helen couldn't play Peekaboo. She was not taught to greet people with "Hi" and "Byebye." She could not imitate the words of her mother, and she would not have known if her mother imitated her. She was deprived of the social play and ritual experience with language.

Along with other investigators of child language (Greenfield and Smith 1976, Dore 1975) we have found that the one-word period is lengthy. For our children, it lasted from four to six months. I do not want to sound precise because the beginnings and endings have fuzzy boundaries. For the greater part of the one-word period, the single words were used for more than one function.

The transition from Stage A, in which a word is used by a child for one kind of speech act or function, to Stage B occurs when the word can be used in more than one type of speech act. For example, on the 12-month tape Allen produced /daedi/ three times, imitating his mother. On the next tape at 12½ months, Allen, hearing his father downstairs in the house, said "/daedi/." In this instance he was *reporting* "daddy" as associated with the vocalization and other sounds from downstairs. Imitations and reports are different speech acts. They are also two of the categories used in the research to classify the function of a mother or infant contribution to their interaction. The first stage of the one-word period lasted for Allen, at most, two weeks—the length of time between tapings. Such was the case for Carol and Joel. It was complicated to judge for Jean, who uttered two words at nine months and then not another word (on the tapes) for the next six tapings. The transition of Stage C, in which words are abstract, occurs late in the one-word period.

Infants do not communicate to parents that they have had an insightful experience, that everything has a name, or that they have cracked the sound-meaning code. Even children as old as three or four years appear unable to think about their use of language in the way Helen Keller reports doing at seven years. For infants between one and two years of age, cracking the sound-meaning code is an unconscious process. A rapid increase in vocabulary or verbalization at 17 to 18 months was observed by Dore (1978) and Nelson (1979) and attributed by them to the infant's unconscious realization that objects have names. When the infant understands, unconsciously, that the speech sounds he or she hears are symbols standing for objects like tables, actions like jumping, and qualities like hot, the infant has cracked the code and can use words to communicate, think, and remember. We may say that, for the infant, words now have meaning as words in the English language.

To summarize what has been said thus far about the course of development of language use by the human infant; the newborn has an innate repertoire of signals including smiling, cries, and babbling. Like animals in contact with human beings, the human infant in interaction with others develops new communicative behaviors. In the kind of environment in which the infants of our research lived, as firstborns and with their mothers as their principal caretakers, infants learn English phonology, first rules of conversation, and requesting gestures. First words are learned as components of gestures and rituals, not as abstract symbols. Then, slowly or suddenly, the child gains the insight that everything has a name, and words become abstract symbols for the child rather than utterances tied to particular gestures or occasions.

THE FUNCTIONAL ANALYSIS OF DISCOURSE

Learning one's native language is a case of learning by doing. People become competent speakers of their native language before they ever get to school. They have learned to speak their language meaningfully and grammatically, in the course of daily interaction with other human beings. Children learn the grammar of their language from the persons with whom they interact. Two-year-olds who interacted with no one older than themselves would gain no more than two-year-old grammatical competence—even when they became four-year-olds, roughly the age when the child raised in an ordinary home situation has mastered the basic grammar of his or her native language. This line of reasoning has led me to the research regarding Allen, Carol, Jean and Joel's development of language. Analysis of the interaction between the infants and their mothers has been the central focus of the research because I believe this is where these children became language users. What was the interaction like and how did it change over time? A crucial decision a researcher makes is deciding on what behaviors or aspects of behavior (variables) to record. The aspects of behavior which seemed most promising as variables were (1) *what* the mother and her infant were doing in interaction with each other, that is, a functional categorization of their behaviors, (2) *how* they were carrying out whatever function a behavior had—by action, vocalizing, or speech, and (3) if the function were being carried out through speech (the behavior which is the central subject of this research), was the speech a one-word utterance, a presyntactic utterance (more than one word but not grammatical), or syntactic speech (an utterance conforming to the rules of English grammar).

Over the first two years of the lives of Allen, Carol, Jean, and Joel we videotaped the infants and their mothers as they went through the same segment of their daily lives—as the babies were undressed, bathed, dried, dressed, played with, and fed by their mothers. Having a constant sequence of events makes it possible to see what is common to the interaction for the four infant-mother pairs and how the interaction of each pair changes over time.

I am going to describe results of this research without explaining how they were obtained; however, methods are described in the appendix to this chapter so that the reader can find out in detail what was actually done to turn what appeared and what was heard on the videotapes into data that could be counted and analyzed to produce empirical findings.

What were the infants and mothers doing in interaction with each other during the times that we videotaped them over the two years? I have said that there was a common scenario for all the videotapings. The baby was undressed, bathed, dried, dressed, played with, and, if there was time left in the half hour taping time, fed. Within this framework, infant and mother emitted behaviors each of which was categorized as to its function.

Before presenting the results of analyzing the functions of the infants' and their mothers' behavior, I need to explain what is meant by the term "criterial for language use" when it is applied to functional coding of behavior. It means that if a person is going to become a competent language user, she will have to be able to perform this (criterial) behavior. Thus *compliance* is a criterial functional behavior. It does not require production of speech. It may not even require speech comprehension. A person (or pet) may understand and comply with a nonverbal directive or command. What makes compliance criterial for language use is that it is a response to a communication that shows comprehension. Participation in nonverbal interactive rituals, even if the ritual involves snorting or squeaking rather than use of language, is behavior criterial for language use because participating in a ritual depends on having learned the conversational rules, one at a time and both get turns, and also how the turn gets passed.

Use of speech is a higher order criterial behavior than compliance, participation in a nonverbal, interactive ritual, or any of the other criterial functional behaviors. Thus, if the child's participation in a verbal ritual like "Peekaboo" is being coded, it is coded as a criterial functional behavior, but also as speech. Because speech is the higher order criterial behavior compared with criterial functional behavior, performing a verbal ritual would contribute to the child's percentage of speech behavior (2) rather than criterial functional behavior (3), as shown in Table 5.1. Use of grammatical speech (1) is the highest order of behavior criterial for language use, and if a child uses grammatical speech then the behavior is coded 1, rather than 2. Using this four dimensional coding system makes it possible to look at Allen, Carol, Jean, and Joel's developing use of language to carry out functions initially carried out without language and to carry out functions impossible without language.

THE FINDINGS

The broad outline of the process is shown in Table 5.1. Over the three periods for all the infants there is a rise and then a fall in criterial functions carried out nonlinguistically. There is a rise in speech and grammatical speech and a decline in noncriterial behavior.

In the prelinguistic period the only means the infants have for producing criterial behavior is functional (except for Jean who produced two words, /ăke/ (ok), and /bābā/ (bottle), on the nine-month tape. Because Jean did not produce another word on the video tape until 12 weeks later, I have not altered the time periods for her. The infants' noncriterial contributions that do not carry out criterial functions are acts and vocalizations. At least 90 percent of all infant contributions are noncriterial behaviors during the prelinguistic period. In the one-word period the percentage of infant behavior that is noncriterial has fallen so that Allen, the infant with the most noncriterial behavior, has 77 percent and Jean, with the least, has 60 percent. Each infant has a small percentage of criterial grammatical behavior in the one-word period ranging from 1 percent for Allen to 7 percent for Jean.

Here is an example of a criterial grammatical contribution:
Jean at 15 months says, "/āy p̄u/" or "I pull." (Jean looks at mother and

TABLE 5.1. Criterial Behavior in the Prelinguistic, One-Word, and Syntactic Periods

		Prelinguistic %	One-Word %	Syntactic %
Allen	0	90	77	56
	1	0	1	9
	2	0	2	33
	3	10	21	2
Joel	0	95	68	40
	1	0	6	5
	2	0	8	46
	3	5	19	9
Jean	0	90	60	31
	1	0	7	9
	2	4	10	57
	3	7	23	4
Carol	0	94	66	10
	1	0	2	20
	2	0	18	69
	3	6	14	0

0 = noncriterial
3 = criterial function
2 = speech
1 = criterial grammar

pulls a sock.) (The children's grammar is discussed in Chapter Seven.) Rarely are grammatically criterial sentences like Jean's contributed by an infant during the one-word period. During the one-word period the percentage of spoken contributions that are not syntactically well formed, or grammatical, varies considerably from infant to infant—from 2 percent for Allen to 18 percent for Carol. The spoken contributions that are syntactically criterial add another 1 percent to Allen's spoken contributions and 2 percent to Carol's. The majority of infants' contributions that consist of criterial behavior are still just functional.

In the syntactic (grammatical) period, the situation has completely changed. The percentage of infant contributions to the interaction that consists of criterial functional behavior is now less than it was in the prelinguistic period for all the infants except Joel, and speech and syntactic criterial behavior are both increasing. The infant's contribution to the interaction has become, for the most part, verbal. The same direction of change over the three periods in type of contribution characterizes each child, but notice that there are great differences in percentages among the four children.

What was the infant-mother interaction like over this period in which the infants became language users? What were they doing and how did their actions reflect the infants' changing linguistic status? The functional analysis of the interactions is the way I have looked at these questions.

Table 5.2 shows all the functions of infants and mothers that account

TABLE 5.2. Principal Functions of Infant and Mother Contributions to Their Interaction

	INFANTS				MOTHERS			
	Allen	Joel	Jean	Carol	Allen	Joel	Jean	Carol
3 mos.[a]	B- NGI Sig. Act Voc. Prac. Express Veg. Noise	B- NGI Sig. Act Voc. Prac. Express B- Non. Compl.	B- NGI Sig. Act Voc. Prac. Express Veg. Noise	B- NGI Sig. Act Voc. Prac. Express Veg. Noise	Express Report A RI Performative Pos. Feed A Ind. Dir.	Express Report A RI Performative	Express Report A RI Performative A RI$_t$	Express Report A RI Performative Pos. Feed Imitation
6 mos.[a]	B- NGI Sig. Act Express Voc. Prac. A Neg. Dir.*	B- NGI Sig. Act Express Voc. Prac. B Compl.*	B- NGI Sig. Act Express Voc. Prac. B- GNI	B- NGI Sig. Act Express Voc. Prac. B- Non. Compl.	Report Express A RI Performative Boundary MSB	Report Express A RI Performative A Ind. Dir.	Report Express A RI A Ind. Dir.	Report Express A RI Pos. Feed A Directive Imitation
9 mos.[a]	B- NGI Express Voc. Prac. Sig. Act Veg. Noises	B- NGI Express B- Non Compl. A Directive*	B- NGI Express Voc. Prac. B- Non Compl. Reference B- GNI	B- NGI Express Imitation* B- NGI$_t$	Express Report A RI Boundary	Express Report A Ind. Dir. Performative Attention	Express Report A RI A Directive	Express Report A RI A Directive Imitation
12 mos.[b]	Express B- NGI Voc. Prac. Sig. Act Non Compl. Compl.*	Express B- NGI Voc. Prac. A Directive*	Express B- NGI Voc. Prac. Sig. Act B- Non Compl. B Compl.*	Express B- NGI Voc. Prac. Sig. Act B- Non Compl. Ritual*	Report A RI A Directive Pos. Feed Express	Report A RI A Directive Express Imitation	Report A RI A Directive Pos. Feed Express	Report A RI A Directive Pos. Feed Performative
15 mos.[b]	Express B- NGI Sig. Act Voc. Prac. A Directive*	Express B- NGI Sig. Act Voc. Prac. A Directive* B Compl.*	Express B- NGI Sig. Act Ritual* B GI*	B- Express B- NGI Sig. Act B Compl.*	Report Express A RI Performative A Ind. Dir. Imitation	Report Express A RI Performative A Directive	Report Express A RI A Directive Sig. Act Pos. Feed	Report Express A RI Performative A Ind. Dir. A Directive

Table 5.2. continued

	INFANTS				MOTHERS			
	Allen	Joel	Jean	Carol	Allen	Joel	Jean	Carol
18 mos.[b]	Voc. Prac. Sig. Act B- Non Compl. B- NGI B Compl.* B GI* Imitation*	Voc. Prac. Sig. Act B- Non Compl. Express Ritual* Report*	Voc. Prac. Sig. Act B- NGI Ritual A Directive* B Compl.* B GI, Report**	Voc. Prac. B- NGI Express B Compl.* Imitation* Reference* Report*	Express Report A RI A Directive A Ind. Dir. Pos. Feed	Express Report A RI A Ind. Dir. Imitation Attention	Express Report A RI A Direct Pos. Feed	Express Report A RI A Direct Pos. Feed Imitation
24 mos.[c]	Express Report* B GI* B- NGI Sig. Act Voc. Prac. Reference*	Express Report* B GI* B- NGI Neg. Feed.*	Express Report* B GI* B- NGI B- GNI Pos. Feed.* B Compl.*	Report* B- GI* Performative* Reference* A Directive*	Report A RI Pos. Feed A Ind. Dir. Boundary Express	Report A RI Pos. Feed A Ind. Dir. Imitation A Directive	Report A RI Pos. Feed A Direct Express	Report A RI Pos. Feed A Ind. Dir. Performative A Directive

[a]Preverbal period
[b]One-word period
[c]Beginning of syntactic speech
A: First term of contingency pair
B: Second term of contingency pair
B-: Failure to complete a contingency pair

*Critical behavior for the development of language use

TABLE 5.2. Functions[1]

1. Directive*	Dir.
2. Indirect Directive*	Ind. Dir.
3. Compliance*	Compl.
4. Noncompliance	Noncompl.
5. Report*	
6. Request for Information*	RI
7. Gives Information*	GI
8. Gives Noninformation	GNI
9. Non Gives Information	NGI
10. Expressive	Express
11. Requests Information, tutorial*	RI_t
12. Gives Information, tutorial*	GI_t
13. Gives Noninformation, tutorial	GNI_t
14. Non gives Information, tutorial	NGI_t
15. Vocal Practice	Voc. Prac.
16. Performative*	
17. Ritual*	
18. Imitations*	
19. Reference*	
20. Positive Feedback*	Pos. Feed.
21. Negative Feedback*	Neg. Feed.
22. Attention Getter	Attention
23. Boundary	
24. Vegetative Noises	Veg. Noises
25. Negative Directive*	Neg. Dir.
26. Mother Gives Information for Baby	MGIB
27. Mother Complies for Baby	MCB
28. Significant Act	Sign Act

[1]Functions are defined, with examples, in the appendix to this chapter.
*criterial function

for at least 5 percent of their contributions at each data point. Functions accounting for at least 5 percent of the person's contributions are *principal* functions. The first thing to notice is how similar the mothers' principal functions are to each others' and over time. Except at nine months, three or four of the principal functions for the mothers are the same. This means they are interacting with their infants from the point of view of their contributions' purpose or function so that there is a great deal of similarity in what the four infants are presented with. Further, with the exception of *expressive,* the mothers' four consistent principal functions consist of behaviors that are criterial for language use in interaction. From our earliest data point at three months, mothers *report* to their infants and *request* information from them at every data point. Beginning at six months, all the mothers except Allen's have either *directive* or *indirect directive* (a more polite way of asking someone to perform an action) as principal functions. What is most significant about these findings is that they imply that mothers treat their infants as competent to participate, functionally, in interaction before it is really so. Further, not only are all the mother's consistently occurring principal functions (except expressives) criterial for language use, the functions are also, for the most part, verbal behaviors. It looks as though these mothers are interacting with the preverbal and then presyntactic children as though they were and had always been competent speakers. Actually, this is only partially true of mother behavior. The other half of the story will be told later. In brief, mothers teach words and word-use part of the time.

Looking now at the infants, it can be seen that they also have a lot in common in the principal functions of their contributions to the interaction with their mothers. Through the 15 months data point infants also have three or four functions in common (except at nine months). *Vocal practice* and *vegetative noises* are the natural functions of their immaturity. The cooing, crying, and distress noises that get coded as expressives in the early months have approximately the same status as vocal practice except that expressives have positive and negative tone while vocal practice is vocalizing with neutral tone. The four infants have *NGI* (does not give information) as a function at all data points until 18 months when Joel does not. All except Carol have NGI at 24 months. Having this category depends on mother having *RI* (requests information). Notice that at 18 and 24 months, infants have both *GI* (gives information) and *NGI*.

The asterisks on infant functions indicate which functions are criterial for language use, and it can be seen that Allen and Joel show the earliest instances of 5 percent or more criterial behavior. A preverbal negative directive produced as principal function by Allen at six months is composed of a protest noise plus a pushing away gesture. Joel's six months criterial principal function is compliance. In response to directives or indirect directives by his mother, Joel has complied often enough so that at least 5 percent of his contributions to the interaction are compliances. Joel is probably responding to his mother's intonation and gestures rather than the verbal content of her utterances. Looking at Joel's mother s contribution at six months, we can see that both directives and indirect directives are among the functions that account for 5 percent or more of her contributions. Mothers generally contribute more units to the interaction than their infants, so it is possible, as in the case of Joel at three months, for the infant to have noncompliance as 5 percent of his contributions and mother not to have directives, indirect directives, or even the sum of the two as 5 percent of her contributions.

The development of criterial functions by the children is not uniform, as can be seen in Table 5.2. At 24 months, there are only two criterial functions that all four children have: Gives Information and Report. Gives Information depends for its occurrence on a request for information by the mother. At 24 months all of Carol's principal functions are criterial behaviors for language use.

The functions *RI*, requests information, and *RI*ₜ, requests information tutorial, are not only functional categories, they are also first terms of contingency pairs. *GI*, gives information, and *GI*ₜ, gives tutorial information, are the second terms in the pairs, expected after *RI* and *RI*ₜ, respectively. As we have said, GI and GIₜ are coded only when a contribution is a response to RI or RIₜ. *NGI*, does not give information, and *GNI*, makes a response which is not an informative answer, are codings used when the discourse fails and the requested information is not forthcoming.

D, directive, and *ID*, indirect directive, are also first terms of contingency pairs for which the expected second term for both is *C*, compliance. *NCOMP*, noncompliance, is coded when the discourse fails. In order to look at the interaction functioning as a discourse, I have marked the occurrence of RI, RIₜ, D, and ID as principal functions with an "A," GI, GIₜ, and COMP with "B," and GNI, NGI, and NCOMP with a "B-." It can be seen that through the two year data point, discourse is asymetric for the four mother-infant pairs. Mothers have only first terms of contingency pairs among their principal functions, and they have approximately the same number of occurrences—Allen's mother, 13; Jean's and Joel's, 14; and Carol's, 15. If a mother had each of the four (RI, RIₜ, D, and ID) each time, the total would have been 28.

Table 5.3 gives the distribution of contingency pair members for the children.

The contributions of the children reflect the fact that they are more likely than not to fail in their discourse responsibilities (the excess of B- compared to B). Except for Jean, there is not such a disparity between first and second terms as principal functions. But compared with the possible total (28) or the average mother total initiations (14), both the children's initiations (A) and completions (B) of contingency pairs are small numbers. If we count the number of Bs and B-s for the four children over the first four data points and the number for the last three data points, we see that the number of Bs increases from 4 to 13 and B-s decrease from 27 to 14. This is a significant change and reflects the fact that, when the infants were older, they fulfilled the responsibility to respond appropriately when response is

TABLE 5.3. Distribution of Contingency Pair Numbers as Principal Functions

	OCCURRENCE OF CONTINGENCY PAIR MEMBERS		
	A (1st term)	B (2nd term)	B- (2nd term not supplied)
Allen	2	4	10
Joel	3	3	9
Jean	–	7	13
Carol	2	3	9

expected better than when they were younger. There is very little change in the total number of infant As, initiation of contingency pairs, over the two periods—from 3 to 5.

In part, the difference in development of criterial behaviors as principal functions for these children reflects differences in their rates of maturation. Allen, at 24 months, continues to have vocal practice and significant acts among his principal functions. Vocal practice indicates that at least 5 percent of his contributions are neutrally toned vocalizations that are *not* potential words. Significant acts are acts that have their significance because the other person in the interaction responds. The significant act is not an intentional contribution to the interaction. When Allen drops the soap, it becomes a significant act because his mother says, "Oh, you dropped the soap." Mothers' respond to their infants as though their behaviors were intended as contributions to the interaction even when they weren't. Significant acts, along with vegetative noises and vocal practice, cease to be a principal function of the infants as criterial behaviors become more frequent.

INDIVIDUAL DIFFERENCES

Allen is not only probably less linguistically developed thtan the other infants, he is different from the other infants in being less interested in the interaction and more interested in objects; he displays interest, for example, in how the faucet works. It is certainly not that Allen is less intelligent than the other children. Allen had had his birthday party about three weeks before the two year videotaping (actually done at two years, three weeks). At one point during the taping, while he was in the tub having his bath, he draped his washcloth over the (rather wide) side of the tub and sat the rubber animals, which were in the tub, around the washcloth. He then caught his mother's eye and said, "/aebi burde duyu" or "happy birthday to you." Allen was engaged in symbolic play decentered from himself, very mature behavior for a two-year-old. But he was not sufficiently mature linguistically to say something like, "See my animals at a birthday party." "Happy birthday to you" was Allen's way of referring to the event he had created.

Following Kathryn Nelson's work (1973), other researchers have also found there are differences in the first 50-word vocabularies of children that reflect language use primarily for social play or to talk about "things," referential language use. Joanne Morse in her master's thesis (1981) has compared the early speech of Carol and Jean and found that, to the 18 month data point, the distribution of their total utterances, Table 5.4, showed a difference like that which Kathryn Nelson had found.

When Joel was two years old, he engaged in a little word game with his mother.

TABLE 5.4. Distribution of Utterances of Carol and Jean (To 18 Months)

	PERCENTAGES	
	Carol	Jean
Social Speech	18	62
Reference	57	16
Request	25	22

Morse 1981

Joel	*Mother*
	1. What does the doggie say?
2. Bow-wow	
	3. What does the kitty say?
4. Meow	
	5. What does the raven say?
6. Never more	

This game has an amusing point for adults, but Joel lacks the experience with Poe's poem, which makes the sequence humorous. Joel loved the game, though, and I conclude that what Joel enjoyed was taking part in a little ritual that made his mother happy with him—a social use for language.

As I think now about the concern of this chapter, how beginning language use develops in the interaction of these infants with their mothers, I am impressed with how much of what goes on is in the nature of lessons in language use. I have to keep reminding myself and readers that children who are not first-born, middle-class infants whose mothers are their principal caretakers also become language users. At the present time, we have not satisfactorily worked through the following issues: how much of the development of language use depends on learning from environmental input and how much is innate, maturationally determined with environmental input needed only in sufficient quantity to trigger a powerful acquisition device located in the human brain?

Appendix:
Methods for the Analysis
of Discourse Development

The data for the analysis of discourse development came from the videotapes of the four infants and their mothers when the infants were 3, 6, 9, 12, 15, 18, and 24 months old. The 3, 6, and 9 month tapes provide data with which to analyze mother-infant interaction for the prelinguistic period; 12, 15, 18 month tapes for the one-word period; and the 24 month tapes provide a sample of interaction for each mother-infant pair when the infants were beyond the one-word period. The periods have slightly fuzzy boundaries. Jean has two words on the 9 month tape, but there is not a single utterance by her on the five subsequent tapes (these latter tapes were not used in this study). The data samples are based on the first 75 infant contributions in the 3, 6, and 9 month tapes (if there were as many as 75); all the mother contributions that go along with the 75 infant contributions and 100 infant contributions and all the mother contributions that go along with these in the 12, 15, 18, and 24 month tapes. With the three sets of data, it is possible to see how the interaction is affected as the linguistic status of the infants changes.

DATA REDUCTION

In order to analyze the videotapes it was necessary to transcribe what occurred on the tapes onto analysis paper. We described acts, transcribed vocalizations, using IPA, and transcribed speech, spelling words out in the English alphabet and punctuating with periods, commas, and question marks. We transcribed events in chronological order, using separate halves of the paper for infant and mother as well as separate columns for infant and mother acts, vocalizations, and speech. If two events occurred simultaneously, they were entered on the same line.

THE UNITS

The units are the contributions of mother and infant to the interaction. A contribution is not the same thing as taking a turn in the interaction because a turn may consist of more than one contribution. For example, at 18 months, Carol is getting undressed for her bath. She has pulled off one sock.

Carol	Mother
1.1. /to/ toe	
1.2. /to/ toe (pulls on other sock)	
	Pull hard. 2
3. (pulls off other sock)	
	Good Girl 4

In this little sequence, Carol has two turns, but she makes three contributions. Contribution 1 and 2 are part of the same turn. Turns are variable in length, but the definitions for contributions make them short and simple in the sense that a contribution does not contain a series of behaviors.

CRITERIAL BEHAVIORS

Each contribution is coded in three different ways: by type, by function, and (if the contribution is verbal) by the structure of the verbalization. The categories for coding type of contribution, function, and structure where the contribution is verbal are described in the next three sections of this appendix.

In general a criterial behavior, although not necessarily a language-using behavior, implies a competence that will be necessary for language use. Criterial behaviors are marked with an asterisk. The criterial *types* of contributions are the two (of 13) categories involving speech by the infant. Criterial *structures* of verbalizations are all syntactically well-formed English sentences. Criterial *functions* are the behaviors learned by the infant that make communicative interaction possible.

TYPES OF CONTRIBUTIONS

There are three types of contribution to the interaction: speech, vocalizations, and acts. The first ten categories are identical sets of five for mother and baby.

Mother	*Baby*
1. speaks	6. speaks*
2. vocalizes	7. vocalizes
3. acts	8. acts
4. speaks/acts	9. speaks/acts*
5. vocalizes/acts	10. vocalizes/acts
11. Mother speaks for baby	13. baby ∅ (null)
12. Mother acts for baby	

The behaviors for type of contribution criterial for language use (marked with an asterisk) are the ones involving speech by the infant. Category 13, baby null, means that the infant did not respond when his mother asked him a question or gave him a directive. These are contributions that require a response.

FUNCTIONS OF THE CONTRIBUTIONS CRITERIAL FOR LANGUAGE USE

The reader may have noticed that, in the discussion of speech acts, I have sometimes spoken of the utterer's meaning of the speech act (as opposed to the syntactic-semantic meaning of the utterance in the English language). At other times I have spoken of the function of the speech acts. For the speech act of requesting, we can call requesting the *utterer's meaning* of the utterance /zís/, or we can say the *function* of the utterance is to make a request. The syntactic-semantic meaning of the utterance in English is just the meaning of *this,* something near. I use the term *function* because acts and vocalizations as well as speech can be analyzed functionally. The functions are:

Directive (or request): "You've got to lift your foot now."; "Open it."; "Come on."; "/m̃/" accompanied by open-handed reach

Negative Directive: refusal gesture accompanied by protest vocalization

Indirect Directive: "Can you help me?"; "Wanna get out?"

Compliance: any act that complies with a directive or indirect directive; for example, Mother says, "Wanna hand me the soap?" and Allen gives Mother the soap

Request for Information: "Does it hurt?"; "Are you hungry?"; "You like that?" "It's not hot, is it?"

Request Information, tutorial (RI$_t$): "What does the kitty say?"; "Where's your nose?"

Gives Information: "Yeah" in response to "You see it?"

Gives Information, tutorial (GI$_t$): after "What does the kitty say?" the child answers, "Meow."

Ritual, Greetings: "Hi"; "ByeBye"; "Peekaboo"; "One shoe off"

Imitation: any word or multiword combination uttered in imitation of the other

Reference: "Man" accompanied by point at toy; "Boat" accompanied by gaze at toy boat

Positive Feedback: verbal, positive response to act or verbalization (not question) of other; for example, "Yes" in response to "the box" or "Good" in response to child's stepping out of pants

Negative Feedback: verbal, negative response; for example, "That's Mommy's" as Joel reaches for brush; "Not that way" as Carol misuses a toy; "No" Joel says in response to "Let's get out, now."

Performative: verbal part of an act; for example, "Here's the whale" said as mother hands toy to child or "Here you go" as mother puts child in tub.

Functions coded that are *not* criterial for language use include non-compliance, expressive, vocal practice, vegetative noises, and significant but nonintentional acts.

SYNTACTIC CATEGORIZATION

Contributions of mother and infant that are verbalizations are given a syntactic coding. The syntactic categories that mark verbal behavior as criterial are all variations of the subject-predicate sentence. There are 23 criterial syntactic categories including (1) simple declarative sentence,* (2) simple question,* (3) complex sentence,* (4) well-formed elliptical sentence,* and so on. Noncriterial, nonsyntactic categories include (1) topic constructions, (2) comment constructions, (3) interjections, (4) vocatives, (5) rituals, (6) poems, and any other rote-learned rather than spontaneously constructed verbalizations.

6

The Linguistic System

When I began my research, I thought that my theory of language development was going to be a theory of language *learning,* that children's language development depended on the language input to them from the competent speakers with whom the children interacted—primarily mothers and other important caregivers. But current research findings in addition to ours indicate that some features of children's language use are better explained as maturationally determined than as dependent on the language spoken to them. As will be seen in Chapter Seven, longer MLU (Mean Length of Utterance) in child speech is associated with a higher proportion of syntactically well-formed grammatical sentences. But there are differences among children in how rapidly their MLU increases, even though there is great similarity in the MLU and other relevant features of the language spoken to them. Such findings suggest that a satisfactory theory of language development is going to consist in part of an explanation of how the inborn characteristics of the human brain and its maturation affect language development.

THE ANATOMY
OF LANGUAGE AND SPEECH

I used to think that human beings had language while other species did not simply because human beings have larger brains and are generally more intelligent than other species. But the evidence is that human brains, unlike the brains of other primates, have elements specialized to process linguistic information; evidence suggests that language use is not simply one of a general set of cognitive (having to do with knowing and thinking) functions that are all carried out in the same way in the brain. A disposition to acquire language use seems to have evolved in human beings, like the disposition in pigeons and other animals to categorize, discussed in Chapter Three. In addition to the disposition to use language, areas specialized to language functions (Broca's and Wernicke's areas) exist in the human brain.

The Brain: Localization and Laterization of Functions

In most human beings the language areas are on the left side of the brain. A diagram of the left side or hemisphere of the brain will make the discussion of language and the brain easier to follow. Figure 6.1 shows the left hemisphere. The brain has two hemispheres approximately the same size and shape, fitted together like the two halves of a walnut. The hemispheres are connected by a bundle of nerve fibers called the *corpus callosum,* a pathway that permits the two hemispheres of the brain to be in communication. The outer surface of the hemisphere is called the *cerebral cortex.* The cortex is the "grey matter" of the brain, grey because it consists of nerve cells. Beneath the cortex is the white matter, mostly nerve fibers that connect the nerve cells of the cortex with other nerve fibers, which finally connect the cortical nerve cells with the nerve cells of sense organs and muscles of the body. The cortex is the part of

FIGURE 6.1. Left hemisphere of the human brain.

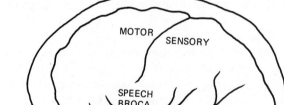

the brain that controls seeing, hearing, and the other senses and exerts voluntary control over the muscles and therefore over the voluntary actions of the body. All involuntary activity like breathing and blood circulation is regulated by subcortical parts of the brain. The sensory and muscular activities of the right side of the body are controlled by the left hemisphere and vice versa because the principal bundles of nerve fibers cross in the brain. Figure 6.1 shows the areas of the left hemisphere where control of particular right-side functions is localized. The area marked *motor,* along the line drawn from the top of the cortex, is the *motor cortex* where all voluntary movements of the right leg, arm, fingers, eye, and so on are controlled. If a person suffers a stroke (a failure of the heart and circulation that causes damage to the brain), and the person's right side is paralyzed, we know that the motor cortex of the left hemisphere was injured by the stroke. Injury to Broca's and Wernicke's areas would interfere with speech production and comprehension respectively. There are no areas in the right hemisphere corresponding to the speech areas. Language is a left-hemisphere function in the great majority of human beings. (Some left-handed people have the language area in the right hemisphere.) As the child develops, the two hemispheres of the brain become specialized for certain functions: language in the left hemisphere along with music and other serial ordered phenomena; spatial orientation and spatial pattern recognition, including recognition of faces, and perception of environmental (nonspeech) sounds (like automobiles, water flowing, and footsteps) in the right hemisphere. We say that these functions are *lateralized* in the brain. As yet it has not been determined when lateralization is complete. Evidence appears when individuals who have had a stroke or sustained a severe head wound on the left side of the head recover. A severe injury or a stroke kills nerve cells of the cortex. These dead nerve cells are not replaced. The human central nervous system, unlike the rest of the human body, does not regenerate cells. We are born with all the nerve cells of the central nervous system that we will ever have. That is the reason why people do not recover CNS functions lost through destruction of nerve cells. A function is recovered only if some other nerves can take over the function. If an individual over the age of two recovers his language functions, then it is inferred that, following the stroke, language functions shifted from left-hemisphere to right-hemisphere control. This shift is possible only if the brain is not yet lateralized. I have seen reports that lateralization is complete as early as age five and as late as puberty. But if lateralization is complete, and some language function was lost with the injury, it is lost for good.

The various impairments in language function are called *aphasias.* Broca's aphasias are difficulties of various kinds in producing speech. Wernicke's aphasias are difficulties in comprehending speech.

Human beings also have a special anatomical link between the auditory (hearing) system and the speech production system. This connection is necessary so that human beings can learn to speak. Infants hear the speech they produce and at the same time get feedback from the movements of their vocal tracts; it is hearing one's speech and getting the muscular feedback at the same time that is necessary in learning to speak.

The Vocal Tract and the Production of Speech Sounds

The part of the body involved in the production of speech includes the lungs, trachea (windpipe), larynx (voice box, which contains the vocal cords), pharynx (or throat), mouth (including tongue, teeth, and lips), and the nose. Altogether, these organs form a tube extending from the lungs to the lips (see Figure 6.2). The upper part, above the larynx, is called the *vocal tract*. If we just breathe out, our breath makes no sound. Speech sounds come from constricting the larynx and vocal tract in various ways. The manner and place in the vocal tract of their production provides the basis for classifying speech

FIGURE 6.2. The human vocal organs.

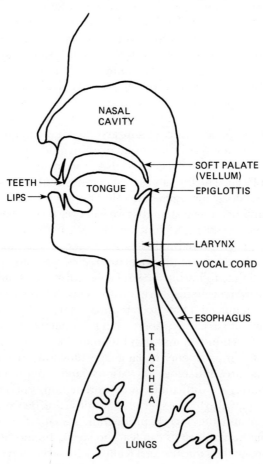

sounds. The easiest way to observe how different speech sounds are produced is to do it yourself.

First, put the tips of your fingers against your larynx (the adam's apple) and make the vowel sound of the *a* in *around;* this sound is called schwa and is written as [ə] in the International Phonetic Alphabet. You will feel your vocal cords vibrate. This is true whenever a speech sound that is voiced is uttered. All vowels sounds are voiced. We will consider the consonants in a moment. Now, instead of [ə], make the sound [i], which is the vowel sound in *meet.* Observe how you have moved your lips, teeth, jaw, and tongue, particularly your tongue and lips. Try [a], the sound of the *a* in *father,* and again you can observe that, in order to produce [a], you have altered the shape of your vocal tract by moving your tongue, lips, and so on. The most important determinants of which vowel will be pronounced are the shape of the tongue, its height in the mouth, and the shape of the lips.

In addition to the pure vowel sounds, there are three diphthongs in American English: [ay], [aw], and [ɔy]. These are also vowels, but they are vowel sounds whose quality changes noticably during production as the positions of tongue, lips, and so on, are altered. This is easiest to hear in the [ɔy], the vowel sound in *boy* and *oyster.* The diphthong [ay] is the vowel sound in *bite,* and [aw] is the vowel sound in *brown.* The vowel sounds used in standard American spoken English are given in Table 6.1.

When a person makes a vowel sound, the air from the lungs is not impeded in its path through the vocal tract and out the mouth. When consonant sounds are made, the passage of air is impeded at various places in the vocal tract and in various ways; this is accomplished mostly by movements of the tongue, teeth, and lips. Consonant production can best be analyzed in terms of the place in the vocal tract and manner in which the sound is produced, and I want to provide a broad description of the consonants in these terms. But first, there is a characteristic of consonants that applies to them all. Some consonants are *voiced* like the vowel sounds, which means that they are produced with enough constriction of the vocal cords to cause them to vibrate. The *voiceless* consonants are produced with no constriction of the vocal cords. The English phonemes /s/ and /z/, /t/ and /d/, /k/ and /g/, and /p/ and /b/ are four pairs in which the two consonants are produced in the same place in the vocal tract and in the same manner except that the first member of the pair is voiceless and the second is voiced. The shape of the vocal tract is the same for both members of a pair. Again, the reader can check this by placing finger tips on the larynx to feel vibrating vocal cords; one can check to see if the first member of each pair is voiceless and the second, voiced. Checking for voicing is somewhat difficult because it is hard to produce a consonant sound all by itself. When we think we are, we have usually appended a shwa, and the sound produced is [tə] or [də]. However, I think it is possible to produce /s/ and /z/ in isolation. See Table 6.2 for the pronunciation of consonants.

If you have tried out the feel of voiced versus voiceless consonants with

TABLE 6.1. The Vowel Sounds of American English
(Written in the Phonetic Alphabet, American Variant)

	VOWELS				DIPHTHONGS
i	beet, rece*i*ve, mone*y*	ʌ	b*u*t, t*ou*gh, *o*ven	ay	b*i*te, d*ie*, *ai*sle
I	b*i*t, cons*i*st, *i*njury	o	b*oa*t, g*o*, thr*ow*	aw	ab*ou*t, br*ow*n, c*ow*ard
e	b*ai*t, r*ay*, inv*ei*gh	ɔ	b*ou*ght, st*a*lk, b*a*ll	ɔy	b*oy*, *oy*ster
ɛ	b*e*t, s*ay*s, *e*nd	a	p*o*t, c*a*r, h*o*nor		
æ	b*a*n, r*a*lly, act*o*r	ə	s*o*fa, *a*lone, s*u*ppose		
u	b*oo*t, d*u*ty, m*o*ve	ɨ	ros*e*s, buss*e*s, crutch*e*s		
ʊ	p*u*t, c*ou*ld, f*oo*t				

the pairs I suggested, you may have noticed that /t/, /d/, /k/, /g/, /b/, and /p/ are all produced by blocking the flow of air from the lungs momentarily and then letting it out in a sudden burst. These consonants are called stop or plosive consonants. Although they have the same manner of articulation, they differ in their place of articulation. To produce /t/ and /d/, the airflow is blocked by placing the tip of the tongue against the inside of the gum of the upper, front teeth. For /k/ and /g/ the tongue is placed against the velum (soft palate). For /b/ and /p/ the lips are closed to block the air flow.

The pair /s/ and /z/ are fricatives. Fricatives are produced by constricting the stream of air from the lungs in the vocal tract. The fricatives /f/ and /v/, for example, are produced by placing the upper front teeth against the top of the lower lip and exhaling the air stream through this constricted space. The nasals like /m/, the sound with which *mother* begins, are produced by blocking the mouth and exhaling the stream of air through the nose. For /m/ the mouth is blocked at the lips. Table 6.2 lists the consonant sounds that are used to construct spoken English words. I am not going to carry through with an exhaustive inventory of place and manner of articulation of English consonants. The reader who wants further information is referred to Fromkin and Rodman (1978) and Denes and Pinson (1973).

WORDS, GRAMMATICAL MORPHEMES, AND SENTENCES

When we discussed the signal systems of animals, in Chapter Two, we found that, in all the studies that have been done, no species has been discovered with as many as 50 discrete signals in its signal system. The chimpanzee, thought to be our closest animal relative, has 13 discrete vocal signals, but these can be further analyzed into 343 intermediate calls in a graded series (P. Marler, as cited by John Bonner 1980). Intermediate calls in a graded series for the Rhesus monkey are described in Chapter Two. Calls are graded in terms of length and intensity. Again making use of the unanticipated jab of a pin as stimulus for a discomfort vocalization by a human being, we can say

TABLE 6.2. The Consonants of English[a]

Manner of articulation	PLACE OF ARTICULATION							
	1 Lips	*2 Lip/ teeth*	*3 Tongue/ teeth*	*4 Tongue/ ridge*	*5 Palate*	*6 Velum*	*7 Lips/ velum*	*8 Glottis*
Nasal	*m* hum			*n* Hun		*ŋ* hung		
Stop	*p* pit *b* bit			*t* time *d* dime		*k* come *g* gum		*ʔ* button
Fricative		*f* fine *v* vine	*θ* thigh *ð* thy	*s* sip *z* zip	*š* sure *ž* azure			*h* help
Glide					*y* yelp		*hw* whale *w* whelp	
Liquid				*l* lane/*r* rain[b]				
Affricate					*č* chunk *ǰ* junk			

[a]Consonants are either voiced or voiceless. The nasals are all voiced. For the others, the consonant in the upper position is voiceless, e.g., *p* is voiceless, *b* is voiced.
[b]*l* and *r* are both voiced, both glides, articulated at tongue/ridge. The difference in their sound is the result of the difference in the shape of the tongue as they are articulated.

63

that a prick of a pin will elicit a short, weak vocalization; a deep jab of the pin will elicit a longer, louder vocalization. The 343 intermediate calls of the chimpanzees reflect more and less intense responses. The 13 discrete signals are coordinated to the different internal sensations of fear, mating urge, hunger, and so on. In contrast, the different words in the adult human vocabulary number in the tens of thousands, and the human child at the time he or she enters first grade knows 8,000 different words (Carey 1978). Furthermore, there is no limit to the number of novel sentences (sentences never heard before) that the human being can produce using his or her store of words and the grammar of his or her language. This last, the infinite productivity of human language, is what we want to understand: what makes it possible for human beings to produce sentences they have never heard before?

Words and Grammatical Morphemes

Frequently friends, including scientists working on the theoretical laws of their own disciplines, have wanted to discuss with me their theories concerning human language. The theory most often suggested to me is that the language system is learned by imitation, or by rote. A learner can learn by imitation or by rote with no understanding of what is being learned, which is also the case when something is learned through conditioning. As we have seen, this is how some elements of human language are learned. The relationship between the sound and the meaning of most words is arbitrary. There is no rule or principle that can be used to explain why we call the four-legged seats with backs that we sit on *chairs* instead of *elephants* or *beds* or *spoons*. The formation of some complex words is rule governed so that, if one knows the meanings of the component words, one can figure out the meaning of the complex word. If one knows *bath* and *tub* or *type* and *writer,* then *bathtub* or *typewriter* can be figured out. But there still remains the fact that the meanings of the component words (*bath, tub, type,* and *writer*) are not rule governed. This aspect of human language, the relationship between the sounds of words and their meanings, is rote-learned. But as soon as the language learner starts to learn that the objects we sit on are actually called *chairs,* there are rules to be learned. As is the case with many rules having to do with human concepts, the rules are not hard and fast. The category of *chairs* has fuzzy boundaries. In general, chairs have four legs, but beanbag chairs do not. In general, chairs are to sit on, but stools and sofas are not chairs. The language learner must learn the general rules that govern language, but also that there are exceptions and irregularities.

The young child, ready to start school, has learned 8,000 words in the normal, day-to-day experience of life. Little children learn words from having the words used in interaction with them. A mother says to her child, "See the doggie," "Pet the doggie," or "Stay away from the doggie; he might bite," as a dog comes on the scene. The mother does *not* say, "Now, I am going to tell you what a doggie is; it has fur, four legs, and a tail." Little children do not learn meanings of the words they know by having the words defined for them. Instead, they induce the meanings of words or the range of objects a word refers to on the basis of hearing the word used in their life experience. This explains why farm children will learn *horse, cow, pig,* and *chicken* at an age when city children have not yet realized that horses, cows, and pigs are not the same kind of animal as dogs (unless they have picture books of farm animals and parents who name the pictures for them). "The experience of children" does not provide a satisfying explanation for their being able to acquire their relatively large vocabularies. Young children appear to be specially able to learn the skills and acquire the knowledge for competent language use. A child frequently does not have to use a word in order to check its meaning. The child unconsciously induces the meaning as he or she hears the word and watches what is going on as it is used. Words referring to salient, concrete objects; vivid, perceptual qualities; and events can be learned readily. The noun *dog,* the adjective *hot,* and the verb *jump* are easy to learn because what they refer to is interesting (or painful) or contrasts vividly with other words. The noun *idea,* the adjective *mean,* and the verb *wait* are harder to learn because what they refer to is abstract. It takes more experience with the use of these words to induce the range of their meanings.

Since the 8,000 word vocabularies acquired by children before starting first grade were learned through life experience, what they refer to has to be important or interesting enough to catch the child's attention so that the word can be associated with its referent. It's easy to understand children's learning *candy, ice cream, naughty, stop,* and *hot.* But something like Helen Keller's reaction to her realization that "everything has a name" must contribute to children's vocabulary growth. Just the realization that things have names may be all that is required for words and their meanings to be learned by the language-prone human child. Children also induce the meanings of grammatical morphemes (the endings on words that indicate plural or past tense) and *functors* ("little" words such as *and, or, a, the, is, in,* and *on*), for example. Children acquire these meanings even though they are much less prominent for learning through experience than the meanings of *sun* and *jump,* which are words referring to an object and an activity that are visible and interesting. Furthermore, children begin acquiring the morphemes as soon as they begin to produce utterances more than one word in length. As will be seen in Chapter Seven, Allen, Carol, Jean, and Joel "sprinkle" grammatical morphemes in their early multiword utterances in a nonsystematic way. Sometimes *'s* appears in an utterance where it is needed, as in "Joel's towel," said by Joel as he points to a towel. But, in the same construction and same context a few minutes later, Joel says, "Joel towel." The errors that young children make in forming plurals or the past tense provide evidence that they induce the rules for forming plurals and past tense rather than learn them by rote or imitation.

1. My foots are warm.
2. My feets are cold.
3. Tommy hurted hisself.

In sentences (1) and (2), the plural of *foot* is incorrect. The correct plural, *feet*, is irregular. The two sentences show that the speaker in each case used /s/ to form the plural. Sentence (1) assumes that the plural of *foot* is like that of all the words that have the regular plural ending. The speaker of the second sentence has learned that the plural of *foot* is irregular but has not quite mastered the irregular form. In sentence (3) the speaker is using the general rule for forming the past tense, written orthographically as "add *ed* to the present tense form." But *hurt* is an irregular verb and has the same form *hurt* in the present and past tenses.

The speaker has formed the third-person reflexive in sentence (3) by using the rule for first- and second-person reflexives—add "self" to the *possessive* pronoun, as in "myself" and "yourself." But the third person rule—add "self" to the *accusative* pronoun, yielding "himself"—is irregular.

Errors like those in sentence (1), (2), and (3) provide evidence that children induce the rules governing grammatical morphemes because it is unlikely that *hurted, hisself, foots,* and *feets* were learned by imitation. Most grownups do not use these incorrect forms, thereby providing them to be learned by imitation. However, imitation cannot be ruled out. The classic experiment of Jean Berko (1958), now Jean Berko Gleason, provided experimental evidence that rule induction rather than imitation is the way children learn the plural, past tense, and other grammatical morphemes. The subjects in her experiment were preschool children. The experiment consisted of eliciting grammatical morphemes from children. In eliciting plurals, Berko first pointed to the picture of an imaginary animal she called the "wug" and said to a child-subject in the research, "Here is a wug." She then pointed to a second picture of two wugs and said, "Now there are two of them. There are two _____."

The child-subject had to supply the missing word, *wug/z/*. Berko found that 76 percent of her preschool subjects could supply the correct plural. They could not have learned the plural by imitation because there is no such animal as a wug. The children could not have heard anyone say, "Look at the wug/z/," as two of them walked by. Using the same technique, Berko elicited plurals for *bik, gutch,* and *tass,* more nouns she invented. Children supplied the correct plurals, *bik/s/, gutch/ɨz/,* and *tass/ɨz/.* When children erred, it was not by supplying the wrong form of the plural inflection but rather by not responding at all. Berko elicited the past tense for verbs she invented—*bing/d/, rick/t/, spow/d/,* and *mott/ɨd/*—and found that 63, 73, 36, and 32 percent of her subjects could supply the grammatical morphemes for the past tense of these invented verbs. Again, when the children erred, it was not through supplying an incorrect morpheme. Errors were all failures to respond.

THIS IS A WUG.

NOW THERE IS ANOTHER ONE.
THERE ARE TWO OF THEM.
THERE ARE TWO _____.

FIGURE 6.3. Wug pictures. (Redrawn from "The Child's Learning of English Morphology" by J. Berko, *Word,* vol. 14, 1958. Reprinted by permission.)

The rules for forming the plural and past tense in English reflect a more general phonological role of English. If a word has a voiced ending, either a vowel sound or a voiced consonant, the grammatical morphemes added for the plural, past tense, or third-person singular, present tense will be voiced, for example, *dove/z/, beg/d/,* and *row/z/.* If the word has a voiceless ending, the added grammatical morpheme will be voiceless. If the word ends with either the voiced or voiceless version of the grammatical morpheme, add the midvowel and the voiced version of the morpheme, for example, *piece/z/, pat/d/,* and *buzz/iz/.*[1]

Sentences

Although some of the aspects of word meaning and word sound correspondence are not rule governed and have to be learned by rote, sentence formation is rule governed, and if one knows the rules for forming sentences, then one can produce sentences one has never heard. In accounting for the adults' ability to produce sentences they have never heard, it might be thought that the rules, grammar, and syntax of adult language were learned in school. But the remarkable fact is that the basic syntax of the language

[1]A more extensive discussion of the phonological basis for the regularity of form of grammatical morphemes is provided by Roger Brown 1973, pp. 282-92.

spoken in the speech community is mastered by children by the age of four years or so. The syntax of their language, those grammatical rules for forming sentences, are induced by children from the language spoken to them. Because four-year-old children have been able to acquire these rules, it should be possible for an adult psycholinguist to figure out what the rules are—as it has been possible to figure out the rule for forming plurals that we have just looked at. Even though four-year-old children induce the basic syntactic rules for sentence formation in their language, it has proved beyond the competence, to date, of any adult psycholinguist to come up with "the set of syntactic rules which will generate all the sentences of a language and no nonsentences." This is the goal proposed by Professor Noam Chomsky of the Massachusetts Institute of Technology for linguistic theorists. We have looked at the rules for forming the plurals and the past tenses in English and now, even though Chomsky's goal has not been reached, we want to present some ideas about the rules for constructing English sentences that take into account their being acquired by young children. It must not be forgotten that rules for constructing sentences are being acquired by children in situations in which language use is a naturally occurring part of the child's interaction with others. If the child is acquiring the syntax of his or her language, it is because the child is interacting with competent speakers.

There is an old story that in bygone days a king raised two infants together, with no one speaking to them, to find out what the original language of human beings was. (There were members of religious fundamentalist sects as late as the nineteenth century who believed it to be Hebrew.) Of course, the infants never learned any language. A twentieth century study has been made by Luria and Yudovich (1971) of twin boys of average intelligence who spent most of their time together with very little contact with anyone besides each other. At age five their speech was primitive and infrequent. They were subsequently placed in separate kindergarten groups. Within three months their language use was on a par with that of the other children in the kindergarten. In order to play with the other children, the twins had to acquire true language. By true language, I mean language that has the syntactic rules of the speech community.

There are grammatical rules in languages that are not acquired by age five. In English we have a verb form called the subjunctive. It is used, for example, when the speaker wants to indicate that the message is hypothetical or contrary to the facts. When Patrick Henry said,

4. If this be treason, make the most of it.

he used the present subjunctive *be* instead of the present indicative *is*. When a person says,

5. If I were you, I wouldn't eat that worm.

he or she is using the past subjunctive forms *were* and *wouldn't*. I think (5) is regularly used by speakers of American English, but (4) has gone out of use since Patrick Henry's time; children no longer hear it and, therefore, do not acquire it. There are other syntactic rules in English that seem to be in the process of falling into disuse. The present subjunctive is just an example. Whatever the rule, if it is not used, it will not be acquired by young children.

The sentences of English and other languages are organized simultaneously into linear and hierarchical structures (Morgan and Newport 1981, Chomsky 1965, Lashley 1951 and others). Linear organization means that there is a correct order for the words of a sentence.

6. The mouse ate the cheese.
*7. Mouse the the cheese ate.
(An asterisk placed before a sentence signifies that it is ungrammatical.)

Sentence (6) has the linear order for an English sentence; (7) does not. Hierarchical organization means that groups of words form separable parts, or constituent structures of sentences.

8. The mouse who lives in my drawer eats cheese.

"The mouse who lives in my drawer" forms a subgroup in sentence (8) which is the same constituent structure of (8) as "the mouse" is of (6). Grammatical sentences in any language can be divided into constituent structures that are shorter than the whole sentence.

If we go word by word through sentence (6) and give the words the names of their syntactic categories, we have:

The	mouse	ate	the	cheese
article	noun	verb	article	noun

and we notice that the sequence, article–noun, occurs twice. We will leave (8) for the time being and cast about for some other sentences that have the same structure as (6).

9.

A	man	chopped	the	wood.
article	noun	verb	article	noun

10. The spider caught a fly.
11. A child drew the picture.

Sentences (6), (9), (10), (11) have the same constituent, syntactic structure even though their meanings are very different. In science we are always on the lookout for underlying regularities, and the regularity we are noticing is the basis for *structural linguistics*. Conventionally in linguistics, constituent structure is spelled out in tree diagrams or rewrite rules (see Table 6.3).

TABLE 6.3. Sentences Separated into Noun Phrase and Verb Phrase

S	
NP	VP
6. the mouse	ate the cheese
9. a man	chopped the wood
10. the spider	caught a fly
11. a child	drew the picture

The letter *S* stands at the top of the tree diagram. It stands for *sentence*. S has two immediate constituents (parts into which the entire sentence can be separated) called noun phrase (NP) and verb phrase (VP).

Sentence (6) has as NP, "the mouse"; sentence (9) has "a man" as NP; (10) has "the spider"; and (11) "a child." Sentence (6) has as VP "ate the cheese." Sentence (9) has as VP, "chopped the wood"; (10) has "caught a fly"; and (11), "drew the picture." The NP, which is one of the two constituent structures into which the entire sentence can be separated, is the *subject* of the sentences. The VP, which is the other part, is the *predicate* of the sentence.

The subject NP and/or the predicate VP can be very complicated; for example, they can contain other sentences, as does the subject NP of sentence (8).

NP and VP are the immediate constituents of S, but they each have constituents themselves. For sentence (6) the constituents of the NP, "the mouse," are two single words—an article (Art) and a noun (N). When the tree diagram gets to the

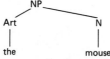

place where the constituents are single words, the constituents are placed directly below their category names and are written as words rather than indicated with "branches." The constituents of the VP, "ate the cheese," are a verb (V) and an NP, which

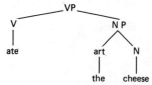

in this case is also formed from an article and a noun.

The tree diagram for sentence (6) is

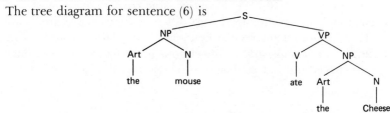

The tree diagram for sentence (8), "The mouse who lives in my drawer eats cheese." is

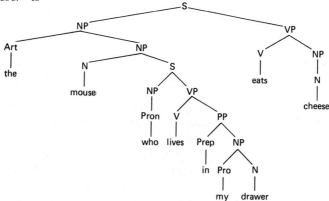

An alternative way to convey information about the constituent structure and hierarchical organization of sentences is by rewrite rules. Rewrite rules "rewrite" the symbols on the right-hand side of the symbol → which stands for "can be rewritten as" until the symbols stand for single words. Rewrite rules convey the same information as the tree diagram. Consider the sentence, "A dog stole the turkey."

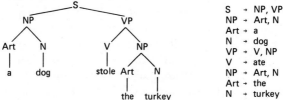

Each rewrite rule corresponds to one of the nodes and its branches of the tree diagram. The rewrite rules start with the rewriting of S into its immediate constituents, just the way one begins to make the tree diagram, and each rewrite rule corresponds to one of the nodes (the symbol to be rewritten) and its branches (what the symbol is rewritten as).

12. Angie bathed the kitten in the fishbowl.

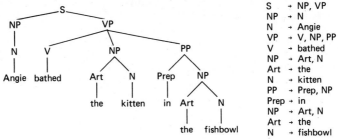

Noun phrase, verb phrase, noun, article, and so on, are all syntactic categories. A syntactic category may contain other syntactic categories, just as NP and VP do. The symbols that label the branches from a node on a tree diagram designate syntactic categories; these are subcategories contained in the syntactic category designated at the node.

All languages have syntactic categories, and the speakers of a language know the syntactic categories of their language, just as they know constituent structure. What is mind-boggling about this fact is that native speakers of a language, including children, have this knowledge without being taught and, in the case of children and some adults, without knowing that they have this syntactic knowledge. We know speakers have this knowledge because the results are observable. Whenever a speaker produces a grammatical sentence (that isn't memorized), the speaker is using the constituent structure rules of the language to produce the sentence.

There is another way of observing speakers' knowledge of the syntactic categories and other aspects of their language's syntax, and that is to question their "grammatical intuitions." In this section on sentences I have been relying on the readers' grammatical intuitions to bring them through the discussion to the conclusion that English sentences do have linear and hierarchical organization.

J. Bresnan has written, "a realistic grammar . . . should contribute to the explanation of the linguistic *behavior* (italics added) and to our understanding of the human faculty of languages" (Bresnan 1978, p. 58). Only such a grammar would be of use for the study of the acquisition of language. Twenty-five years ago, Roger Brown published an experimental study (reprinted, Brown 1970), which provides evidence that syntactic organization determines how utterances will be understood by children. Brown invented three nonsense words, *niss, sib,* and *latt.* He used these in connection with sets of pictures to see if the way he used the nonsense word as verb, mass noun, or count noun in describing the pictures would determine the meaning for the word induced by the children.

> The first picture shows a pair of hands performing a kneading sort of motion with a mass of red confetti-like material, which is piled into and overflowing a blue and white striped container that is round and low in shape. The important features of the picture are the kneading action, the red mass, and the blue and white round container. The motion would ordinarily be named with a verb (like *kneading*), the mass with a mass noun (like *confetti*), and the container with a particular [count] noun (like *container*). . . . Each of the remaining three pictures of this set exactly reproduce one of the three salient features of the first picture, either the motion, the mass, or the container. In order to represent the motion a second time it was necessary also to show a mass and a container. However, the mass was here painted yellow so as not to duplicate the original, and the container was of a different size, shape, and color from the original. The other two sets of pictures involved different content but always an action, a mass substance, and a particular object. In one case, the first picture showed hands cutting a mass of cloth with a strange tool. In the third set, hands were shown emptying an odd container of a slushy sort of material (Brown 1970, p. 23).

The children were shown the first picture in conjunction with one of the nonsense words identifiable either as a verb, a mass noun, or a count noun.

Then they would be shown the remaining three pictures of the set and asked to point out again what had been named in the first picture.

If the nonsense word was to function as a verb, the experimenter would say, "Do you know what it means to sib? In this picture (the first picture described above) you can see sibbing. Now (showing the other three pictures) show me another picture of sibbing." If the word were to function as a count noun, the experimenter asked, "Do you know what a sib is?" If the word were to function as a mass noun, the experimenter asked, "Have you every seen any sib?"

Each of the preschool children in the experiment saw all three sets of pictures and heard each of the nonsense words—one used as a count noun, one as a mass noun and one as a verb. Results are presented in Table 6.4.

This experiment is a beautiful demonstration that preschool children use syntactic information. Syntactic categories like verb, count noun, and mass noun are recognized by preschool children because of the set of operations in which they participate. Brown marked *sib, niss,* or *latt* as a verb by putting the nonsense word in an infinitive construction when he asked, "Do you know what it means to sib (or to niss or to latt)? Only verbs can be operated upon to produce infinitive constructions. He then said, "In this picture you can see sibbing (or nissing or latting)?" thereby producing the present participle construction of the verb. Thus he carried out, in instructing his subjects, two syntactic operations on a nonsense word (for any particular subject only one of the three nonsense words was used as a verb) in which only a verb can participate.

The remaining two nonsense words were used in the syntactic construction, NP, in which only nouns can participate. When the nonsense word was used as a count noun, Brown said, "Do you know what a sib (or a niss or a latt) is?" He made *sib* the noun following the article *a* in the NP in the predicate of the sentence. When the nonsense word was used as a mass noun, Brown asked, "Have you ever seen any sib (or any niss or any latt)? Again he made the nonsense word the noun in an NP. The nonsense words count as mass or count nouns, depending on whether they follow *any* or *a.* Only count nouns can follow the indefinite article *a,* while mass nouns follow quantifiers such as *any.*

This experiment by Roger Brown provides evidence for the "psychological reality" of syntactic categories. The preschool children in this

TABLE 6.4. Picture Selection for Words Belonging to Various Parts of Speech (Syntactic Categories)

Category Depicted	Verbs	Count nouns	Mass nouns
actions	10	1	0
objects	4	11	3
substances	1	2	12
no response	1	2	1

Brown 1970

experiment interpreted the nonsense words as verbs, count nouns, or mass nouns, depending on the syntactic operations he carried out with the nonsense word. I doubt whether the children had ever heard the words *verb* and *noun,* much less knew what they are in the sense of being able to define them. But the children's grammatical or syntactic intuitions caused them to use the nonsense words as belonging to the syntactic category appropriate to the syntactic operations in which Brown made the nonsense word participate.

It would be gratifying if the discussion of sentences and syntax could be concluded on this upbeat note, but unfortunately there are issues regarding the syntax of sentences that a constituent structure grammar is inadequate to deal with.

NEGATIVES AND INTERROGATIVES AND TRANSFORMATIONAL GRAMMAR

English-speaking children's development of the ability to produce syntactically correct interrogatives is not explained by a constituent structure grammar. This development is part of the syntactic competence displayed by preschool children, so it is not a minor matter.

13. Where did you put my skis?

For (13) S cannot be rewritten as NP, VP as it can for the sentences discussed in this chapter. The power of transformational grammars to provide an analysis of the structure of interrogative sentences (as well as negatives and passives) made it attractive for students of child language like me. One of the most impressive demonstrations of the power of transformational grammar to explain the acquisition of syntax by young children is Brown and Hanlon's analysis of the acquisition of negative and interrogative forms. They demonstrated that for the three children studied the order of acquisition corresponded to the transformational complexity of the form (Brown and Hanlon 1970). More will be said about transformational grammar at the conclusion of this description of the development of the child's ability to produce negatives and interrogatives.

It has been shown (Klima and Bellugi 1966) that children's abilities to produce syntactically well-formed negative and interrogative sentences in English develop together. This is not surprising since control of the system of auxiliary verbs is necessary (but not sufficient) for syntactically correct negatives and interrogatives. There are two basic types of interrogatives, yes/no questions and *wh* questions. Yes/no questions are those which can be answered by a "yes" or "no."

14. Have you any gum?
15. Is it sugarless?
16. Can I have a piece?

Wh questions begin with the interrogative words: what, where, when, who, why, and how.

17. What are you thinking?
18. How are you getting to the concert?

In Klima and Bellugi's analysis, in the earliest stage of development questions are marked by intonation for yes/no questions and the *wh* words *what* and *where*. Negatives are marked by *no,* or *not* either preceding or following the rest of the utterance.

19. No a boy bed
20. Wear mitten no
21. See hole?
22. What dat?
23. Where kitty go?

In the second stage children add the words "don't" and "can't" to their negative vocabulary, and they include negatives within utterances instead of placing them at the beginning or end of the utterance.

24. That no mummy
25. Don't bite me yet
26. I can't see you

Second stage interrogatives include:

27. You can't fix it?
28. See my doggie?
29. Why you smiling?
30. Where my mitten is?

They tend to be longer than first stage interrogatives, to include "why" as a *wh* word, but are not more developed structurally than the interrogatives of stage one.

In the third stage, children have mastered the auxiliary system. They produce sentences in which the positive verbal auxiliaries "can," "do," and "will" appear as well as the negatives, "can't" and "don't."

31. Oh, did I caught it?
32. Will you help me?
33. What he can ride in?

On the basis of the examples provided by Klima and Bellugi we would say that mastery of the copula and irregularities in verb tense is not complete but that the glaring failure at stage three is to correctly form *wh* questions. All of Klima and Bellugi's examples are similar: The *wh* word is correctly preposed in the interrogative, but the subject NP and first auxiliary are not interchanged. Transformational grammar provides an explanation. Two transformations are involved in producing *wh* questions as opposed to one for yes/no questions. Children's competence at the third stage makes one transformation possible but not two and transformational theory requires that if the transformation which preposes *wh* words is required it is applied before that which interchanges subject NP and first auxiliary.

I do not believe it worthwhile to provide an account of transformational grammar. It would require an extensive presentation to lay out the analytical apparatus. Instead, a brief sketch meant to acquaint the reader with the kind of insights about the relationships among sentence types that the theory captures and the most general indication of the structure of the grammar follow.

It is clear that the sentences

34. Mick Jagger is singing a song.
35. What song is Mick Jagger singing?
36. What song is being sung by Mick Jagger?

are related to each other. It has not proved possible, using a constituent structure grammar, to give a theoretically useful account of the relationship. For 15 years or so it looked as though the transformational grammar developed by Professor Noam Chomsky of Massachusetts Institute of Technology might be that grammar that would "generate all the sentences of a language and no nonsentences" and account for facts like the relationship between (34), (35), and (36), as well as the production by children of sentences like (33). In transformational grammar there are two kinds of rules, the rewrite rules we have been discussing and transformational rules that explain, among other things, how (34), (35), and (36) are related to each other. They are related by transformational rules that change the word order in a sentence and add and delete words. Transforming a sentence like (34) into (35) requires transformations that change the order of the words in (34), delete *a,* and add the interrogative pronoun *what* in its place so that the NP, *a song,* becomes the NP, *what song.* Transforming (35) into (36) requires transformations, in addition to these required to transform (34) into (35), that change the verb from the active voice to the passive. Transformations change *singing* into *being sung,* change the word order so that *Mick Jagger* follows the verb in (36) and add the word *by* before *Mick Jagger.*

Using transformational grammar it is possible to account for children's regularly producing sentences like (33) in the course of their acquisition of the interrogative

37. What can he ride in?

is derived from

38. He can ride in something.

in the following way: What, the interrogative form of something, is substituted in (38) to produce

39. He can ride in what?

The interrogative word, what, is preposed, transforming (39) into

33. What he can ride in?

Klima and Bellugi's example of a third stage interrogative with *wh* word. Finally,

37. What can he ride in?

is derived from (33) on the basis of a transformation that interchanges the subject NP and first auxiliary to produce interrogative word order.

The account I have just given is only meant to convey the idea of transformations; it is not a rigorous account. In order to have a useful theory, there have to be strong, independent motivations for the transformations. If every time the linguist wanted to explain how one sentence was related to another he invoked a transformation that did not explain anything beyond the relationship of the two sentences at hand, the resulting theory would be loaded with ad hoc rules.

Despite the insightfulness of transformational grammar, there are profound difficulties with the theory—difficulties so grave that linguists have begun to think about other kinds of theories to supplement constituent structure grammar. At this time there is no theory to take the place of transformational grammar, although many linguists are attempting to work out such a theory.

7

After the
One-Word Period

In Chapters Four and Five we considered the beginnings of language development in the human infant. Some of these developments have to do with becoming able to produce intentionally a sequence of speech sounds to form an English word; others have to do with learning to take a turn and participate in a social interaction. Still others have to do with the use of words to carry out intended functions or, as J. L. Austin (1962) put it, "how to do things with words." Chapter Six dealt with English as a linguistic system and with our (incomplete) understanding of the structure of English sentences.

In this chapter we will begin by describing Allen, Carol, Jean, and Joel's early speech.

PUTTING WORDS TOGETHER

At two, Allen, Joel, and Jean had MLUs (Mean Lengths of Utterance)[1] of 1.8; Carol had an MLU of 2.5. Carol was acquiring language at a faster rate than the other three children as measured by mean length of utterance. Although there are other characteristics of language use that are more interesting than MLU, we calculate MLU because it is a simple "overall" measure to calculate and reflects fairly well the grammatical complexity of the language used by the speaker. It takes a longer utterance to say, "I do not like school" (five words) than, "I like school" (three words), and a negative sentence is grammatically more complex than an affirmative sentence. "I want orange juice" (four words), an NP, VP sentence, is grammatically more complex than "juice," a one-word utterance. Table 7.1 shows the distribution by length of

---

[1]MLU is calculated in the following way: all single words count one. *Wanna, gonna,* and *hafta* each count two. Subject plus contracted auxiliary counts two: *I'll* go, *He's* mine.

TABLE 7.1. Distribution of Children's Utterances by Length at Two Years

Length of utterance	ALLEN		CAROL		JEAN		JOEL	
	%S	%N	%S	%N	%S	%N	%S	%N
1	47		30		63		46	
2	3	30	7	9	2	13	6	22
3	9	9	20	12	8	4	2	19
4	1	3	12	4	5	2	2	2
5		1	6			1		
5+					1	1		
	13	42	45	25	17	22	11	44

S = syntactically well formed
N = not well formed
No attempt has been made to determine the syntactic status of one-word utterances.

distribution of utterances that are not well formed. A well-formed utterance is one that is syntactically correct in a two-person, face-to-face conversation; even if standing alone, the utterance would not be syntactically correct. In isolation, only complete sentences are syntactically correct. When Carol's mother said to Carol, as they were playing with a hammer and balls,

1. Mother: You would like me to hit the pink one?
2. Carol: With the hammer.

Carol's utterance is well formed. It is a prepositional phrase that forms part of an answer to her mother's question when the rest of the answer is not explicit but understood on the basis of the mother's question. Carol's utterance is a *linguistic ellipsis,* well formed because the syntactically correct sentence can be constructed from Carol's and her mother's utterances, using the rules of English grammar.

In Carol's mother's utterance change *you* to *I* and *me* to *you* to reflect the change in speaker; then add "with the hammer," yielding Carol's implied sentence, "I want you to hit the pink one with the hammer."

In analyzing the syntax of the utterances of the children at two years, I have not included one-word utterances because it is too difficult to decide whether they are syntactically well formed or based, for example, on a response tendency to answer the mother in a particular way. Responding with no to the question, "Do you want to get out?" does not necessarily mean that the answer is an ellipsis of "No, I don't want to get out."

It can be seen in Table 7.1 that Carol and Jean have approximately the same percentage of multiword utterances (25 percent and 22 percent) that do not conform to all the rules of English grammar — as do Allen, 42 percent and Joel, 44 percent. I would expect from this that Carol and Jean would also have roughly the same percentage of syntactically well-formed utterances— as do Allen, 13 percent, and Joel, 11 percent. However, Jean has the highest children's well-formed sentences in a sample of utterances (approximately the first 100) taken from their two year videotapes. Table 7.1 also shows the percentage of one-word utterances. This is probably the result of the kind of conversation Jean's mother engages in with Jean.

Most intriguing in Table 7.1 is the coexistence in the samples of grammatical and ungrammatical utterances. The presence of a verb in an utterance is essential to its being well formed in English, unless the utterance is a well-formed, linguistic ellipsis, such as "with the hammer." Many of the children's multiword utterances that are not syntactically well formed as English sentences lack verbs. They are like the verbless sentences of topic-prominent languages (Li and Thompson 1976) in having topics and comments rather than subjects and verbs; however, topic does not necessarily come first in the children's utterances as it does in the sentences of topic-prominent languages.

Here are some of the children's sentences broken down into topic and comment:

		Topic	Comment
1.	water that way	water	that way
2.	no water out	water	no out
3.	that way top	top	that way
4.	more tile		more tile

We have already discussed the finding that the first rules, not having to do with producing speech sounds that infants learn in interaction with their mothers, that will have a relation to language use are (1) one person at a time (2) both persons get a turn and (3) rising intonation on the end of an utterance means that the discourse is not finished. These are conversation or discourse rules. *Topic* is a discourse category while *subject* is a syntactic category of sentences. Thus, it seems reasonable to me that topics rather than subjects should figure in the earliest utterances of children. If topics rather than subjects figure in the earliest utterances of children, comments will also, since it is by a comment that something is said about a topic. An important difference between topic-comment utterances and subject-verb sentences is that topic-comment utterances are not governed by the syntactic rules by which sentences with subjects and verbs are constructed. Topic and comment are discourse related. Topics are always definite, and this is so for young children interacting with their mothers. In these interactions the talk is of the ongoing activity—the objects and events that both can see and share. One-word utterances can be related by the child to what is going on. A child's utterance may be a comment on an understood topic as when Joel, just having been put into his bath says, "cold." A child's utterance may be a topic as when Allen, looking at a toy that has fallen into the water, says, "man." I do not want to claim that all one-word utterances can be interpreted in this way.

The majority, perhaps, even though they are definite nouns that look like topics, or adjectives or verbs that look like comments, are not obviously being related to some contextual feature to form a topic-comment structure, partly verbal, partly nonverbal.

Topic-comment is a useful structural description of children's pre-syntactic utterances. With the exception of greetings, interjections, and rituals, all of the children's utterances can be classified as topics, comments, or topic-comment combinations. These are discourse categories rather than sentence categories and, in the early stages of language development, what the children appear to be learning are discourse and phonological rules rather than syntactic rules for forming English sentences. The phonological rules—how to produce sequences of speech sounds to form English words—are essential if the infant is going to be able to use speech to communicate. The discourse rules for topics and comments make it possible for the child to participate using speech in a nonritual interaction with another person. The earliest mastered discourse rules governing turns and how to pass them make orderly interaction possible. Being able to produce topics and comments and then topic-comment combinations when one wants to make it possible to converse meaningfully. Without the incentive of being able to exchange meaningful contributions in interaction using language and the knowledge and information so gained, it does not seem possible that syntax would be learned. For example, when Joel said, "Quito bite leg," and his mother replied, "Mosquito bite on your leg?" she indicated that what he had said was meaningful to her. At the same time she added a bit of English grammar, although not enough to make a syntactically well-formed English sentence that could stand alone, like "There's a mosquito bite on your leg?" But the close match of her utterance to Joel's provides a small amount of information about English grammar and small amounts are more assimilable than large amounts. Joel's mother's utterance was still a topic-comment utterance, but it provided a model closer to an English sentence than Joel's utterance.

EVIDENCE THAT WORD-TEACHING IS ELICITED FROM MOTHERS

I became alerted to the possibility that mothers may instinctively provide appropriate language lessons to their infants by Allen, Carol, Jean and Joel's mothers' vocalizing behavior (Chapter Four). When I went over the 18 month interactions with the idea in the back of my mind that language teaching might have been elicited from the mothers, I was struck by the difference between their verbalizations that were responses to their infants' (one-word) verbalizations and their other verbalizations. (At the same time I noted that the infants' one-word utterances did not make very interesting contributions to the conversation.) Tables 7.2 and 7.3 present samples of the 18 month interaction between Carol and her mother and Joel and his

TABLE 7.2. Carol, 18 Months

Turn	Contribution	Carol	Turn	Contribution	Mother	Mother Response Category
(1)	1	(Carol sits)	(1)	1	You want to take a bath?	Other
				2	Sit down	Other
				3	And we'll take your shoes off.	Other
(2)	2	Toe	(2)	4	That's right.	Other
				5	Ok	Other
(3)	3	(Carol pulls sock)	(3)	6	Toe	Says again
				7	Pull your socks.	Other
(4)	4	Toe	(4)	8	That's a girl.	Other
	5	Toe? (points to other foot)				
			(5)	9	Where is your other Toe?	Frame
				10	Must be inside there.	Continue
				11	Huh?	Continue
(5)	6	Toe	(6)	12	Yeah	Pos. Feedback
(6)	7	knee?	(7)	13	This one's the knee.	Frame
				14	Right	Pos. Feedback
(7)	8	Toe	(8)	15	Pull hard.	Other
	9	Toe (pulls on other sock)				

Table 7.2. continued

Turn	Contribution	Carol	Turn	Contribution	Mother	Mother Response Category
(8)	10	(Pulls other sock off)				
(9)	11	Up (as dress goes over head she raises arms)	(9)	16	Good girl	Other
(10)	12	/duwi/ (looks at diaper)	(10)	17	Up	Says again
				18	Ok	Other
			(11)	19	Yes	Pos. Feedback
				20	You have a duty.	Frame
				21	Right	Pos. Feedback
				22	Come up here so we can take your diaper off.	Other
(11)	13	No				
(12)	14	No	(12)	22	No	Says again
			(13)	24	No what?	Req. Clar.

TABLE 7.3. Joel, 18 Months

Turn	Contribution	Joel	Turn	Contribution	Mother	Mother Response Category
(1)	1	Hot	(1)	1	That's the way.	Other
			(2)	2	Hot	Says again
				3	That was hot.	Frame
				4	Wasn't it?	Continue
				5	I had it too hot before.	Frame
(2)	2	Hot	(3)	6	If you wait just a minute, you can get right in the bath tub.	Changes subject
(3)	3	/be/ bath	(4)	7	Let's have this foot.	Changes subject
				8	Can I have this one?	Other
(4)	4	Hot	(5)	9	Hot	Says again
				10	Here	Other
				11	I'd like to take your shirt off.	Other
				12	But in order to do that, you're going to have let go of that.	Other
				13	It's going to be real cold on your tummy, Honey.	Other
				14	Pull down that arm.	Other
				15	Ok	Other
				16	Mommy didn't do very well in this — with this shirt.	Other
				17	It's too small already	Other

Table 7.3. continued

Turn	Contribution	Joel	Turn	Contribution	Mother	Mother Response Category
(5)	5	Cold				
(6)	6	uhoh (Joel is pouring out water)	(6)	18	Yeah	Pos. Feedback
				19	It is	Continue
				20	Whoops	Other
(7)	7	(Joel switches hands)	(7)	21	Give me your hand	Changes subject
				22	Here, can you take that in the other hand?	Other
(8)	8	Tries to pull	(8)	23	That's a good boy	Other
				24	Now here (pulling up Joel's shirt)	Other
				25	Pull it down.	Other
(9)	9	(Joel tries to pull hard)	(9)	26	Oh	Other
	10	Oh		27	You have to pull hard cause it's pretty tight.	
(10)	11	Tight	(10)	28	Oh	Says again
	12	Tight		29	You're stuck.	Continue
			(11)	30	Tight	Says again
				31	It's tight.	Frames
				32	Ok	Other
				33	Let's get this over your nose.	Other

mother. These samples are presented so the reader can get a sense of the interaction because I use all the 18 month interaction data (and the 24 month data) to test the hypothesis that language lessons are elicited by the infants' one-word utterances.

In the 18 month interaction of Carol and her mother (Table 7.2) Carol produces 11 one-word utterances as she takes 12 turns in the interaction with her mother. (Carol's contributions 4 and 5, and 8 and 9 account for two rather than four turns.) Carol's mother produces 24 utterances, taking 13 turns. Fifty-six percent of Carol's mother's utterances that immediately follow an utterance of Carol's are also one-word utterances while only 33 percent of the mother's utterances that do not immediately follow Carol's are one-word. The corresponding MLUs for the mother are 2.1 and 3.6.

Joel produces nine utterances in taking ten turns, Joel's mother produces 33 utterances in 11 turns. Joel's mother responds to the one-word utterances of her infant with one-word utterances 63 percent of the time. In her third, fourth, and seventh turns, Joel's mother does not respond to Joel's utterance; instead, she changes the topic. Joel's mother's MLU in utterances that immediately follow an utterance of Joel's is 3.5. Her MLU for her other utterances is 5.3. When the mother's contributions are immediately follow-ing direct, verbal responses to Joel's and Carol's one-word utterance at 18 months, they are not only short, but they frequently consist of an imitation of the child's word or of a reinforcing "yeah" or "right."

It appears that mothers credit their children with the ability to understand utterances longer than one word and that the children do so. See the part of Joel's 18 month sample that begins with mother contribution 21, "Give me your hand," and ends with mother contribution 23, "That's a good boy." Also note the part of Carol's 18 month sample that includes mother contributions 7 and 8.

A sample of Joel's and his mother's two year interaction is qualitatively different from the 18 month interaction (Table 7.4). It seems to me more natural and with less of the flavor of a language teaching occasion. Joel and the three other infants are past the one-word period at two years. Their MLUs are no longer 1.0. Does this affect their mothers' behavior? Recall (Chapter Four) that mothers' vocalizing increased relative to their speaking to their infants during the infants' first nine months to one year of life and then decreased. I proposed that vocalizing by the mother was elicited by the infants' behavior and was appropriate to the infants' stage of linguistic development. In the first year of life the infants need to gain control over their vocal tracts and respiratory apparatus so as to be able to intentionally produce speech sounds. Subsequently infants need to learn to intentionally produce speech sounds in sequence to form words and to produce them with appropriate intonation to perform the speech act they intend (Chapter Five). If infant language behavior elicits language behavior from the mother appropriate to the infant's current language development task, mothers

TABLE 7.4. Joel, 2 Years

Turn	Contribution	Joel	Turn	Contribution	Mother	Mother Response Category
			(1)	1	Can you push it in?	Other
(1)	1	(Joel fastens belt with mother's help)				
			(2)	2	There	Other
				3	That's all.	Other
				4	That's all.	Other
				5	Now let's see what's in that bathtub?	Other
(2)	2	Yeah		6	Maybe there's some nice toys to play with in there	Other
			(3)	7	And some water.	Continue
(3)	3	No				
			(4)	8	No	Says again
(4)	4	Quito bite leg				
			(5)	9	Mosquito bite on your leg?	Frames
(5)	5	Yeah				
	6	Quito bite				
			(6)	10	Well it's hard getting squito bites inside (unintell)	Frames
(6)	7	Lay there (wants to push mother down)				
			(7)	11	Well then	Other
				12	Lying down?	Continue
				13	How can we take a bath lying down?	Continue
(7)	8	Lying dere				
			(8)	14	Joel's gotta lie down too	Continue
				15	I wanna see Joel lie down too	Continue
(8)	9	(Joel comes and lies down next to mother)				

(9)	10	Goodnite		(9)	16	Ok	Other
(10)	11	(bangs head on floor)		(10)	17	Goodnite	Says again
(11)	12	(Laugh)		(11)	18	Oops	Other
					19	Boom	Other
(12)	13	Dada		(12)	20	(Laugh)	
(13)	14	Goodnite		(13)	21	How can you take a bath like this?	Changes subject
(14)	15	Sleep Tite		(14)	22	Goodnite	Says again
(15)	16	Nite nite		(15)	23	Sleep tite	Says again
(16)	17	No No		(16)	24	Nite nite	Says again
					25	Oh Joel, you're too much.	Other
(17)	18	No Pamper off		(17)	26	You're too much. (mother starts to take Pamper off)	Other
(18)	19	Uh no (pushes away)		(18)	27	Let's take the Pamper off.	Continue
					28	You don't wanna take the Pamper off?	Continue
(19)	20	In it? (touching box of tiles in bathroom closet)		(19)	29	We can take the Pamper off lying down.	Continue
(20)	21	Out, out (starts to pull tiles out of box)		(20)	30	It's got tiles in it.	Frames

should be reinforcing word use as the infant becomes competent to produce a sequence of speech sounds. Then, as the infants begin to produce multiword utterances, the language behavior elicited from the mothers should change again, perhaps to reinforce and teach multiword use.

In order to test for the effect of the infants' language behavior in the one-word period and when they produced multiword utterances on their mothers' language, I compared the interactions for the four infants and their mothers when the infants were 18 months old and were all in the one-word period with the two year interactions when the infants were all beyond the one-word peiod.

I worked out a system to categorize mother utterances for assessing change or lack of it. Some of the categories are ones that would be expected in any system to classify contributions to a conversation. The three purely conversational categories in the system I have devised are:

1. *Continue*—the mother responds to the child's verbalization in a nonteaching way so as to continue the topic being discussed. (I have indicated at the right column of Tables 7.1, 7.2, and 7.3 the response categories of the mother utterances to provide examples for the categories I describe.) Carol's mother's contributions 10 and 11 are *continue*.

2. *Changes the subject*—the mother's response immediately following a child verbalization is to change the subject. Joel's mother's contributions 6 and 7 in the 18 month sample *change the subject*.

3. *Other*—the mother's utterance is not related to the current subject, which has been spoken about by the child. *Other* includes interjections, remarks concerning the child's appearance or behavior, and remarks about the mother's own agenda.

The remaining four categories are less conversational; they are more appropriate as teaching responses:

4. *Says again*—any mother response that consists of just her child's previous utterance. *Says again* must be the same word or words the child has just used except for pronoun shift; for example, Jean says, "my ball," and Mother says, "your ball." Intonation and speech act function may differ.

5. *Frames*—this category includes expansions like "Mosquito bite on your leg," and incorporations; for example, Carol says, "Toe," and Mother says, "Where is your other toe?"

6. *Positive Feedback*—mother responds to a child verbalization with *yeah, right,* and so on. This must be in the mother's turn, following the child verbalization, with no new subject interpolated, that is, the mother's *yeah* or *right* must be in response to the child's verbalization and not to an act by the child. *OK* is frequently used by mothers as a boundary marker, to indicate

that an activity has been completed or a new one is going to start. Carol's mother's *OK* in Table 7.2 is a boundary marker. Carol's clothes are off, except for her diaper, and her mother is ready to take off the diaper.

7. *Request clarification*—these are "what?" and "huh?" responses to infant verbalizations. I've saved request clarification for last because it can be a category in an ordinary conversation as well as a teaching category. It indicates that the hearer could not understand the speaker's utterance and requests another, more understandable utterance. So even in an ordinary conversation, unless deafness or a loud noise has interfered with the hearer's comprehension, request clarification asks the speaker to improve his or her performance, a teaching response. In the interaction samples of Allen, Carol, Jean, and Joel and their mothers, *request clarification* is very infrequently used—twice at 18 and 24 months by Carol's mother, twice at 18 and four times at 24 months by Jean's mother, once at 18 months by Joel's mother, and twice at 24 months by Allen's mother.

In order to analyze mother responses I separated each mother's responses at 18 and 24 months into those (1) that immediately followed a one-word utterance of her infant and (2) that are the mother's second verbalization after a one-word utterance of her infant. I also separated mother's responses at 24 months that are (3) the mother's first response and (4) the mother's second response following a multiword utterance of her infant. There were so few multiword utterances by the infants at 18 months that I did not analyze mother response to them. I separated mother responses in this way because it seemed probable that a teaching response would more closely follow a child's utterance than would other responses; therefore, the mother's first and second responses seemed the ones to analyze. I separated responses following one-word and multiword utterances on the hypothesis that mother teaching responses elicited by one-word utterances would be fewer when the infant was 24 months old than 18 months old and teaching responses elicited by multiword utterances would be more frequent at 24 months than teaching responses elicited by one-word utterances at 24 months.

I wanted to see whether mother responses to the infants' one-word verbalizations would look more like language lessons at 18 months and more like conversation at 24 months. At the same time I wanted to see whether it would look as though mothers' responses to their infants' multiword utterances at 24 months were primarily teaching responses, rather than conversational responses. I grouped the teaching responses—says again, frames, positive feedback, and request clarification—to compare the percentage these four teaching categories were of all seven categories with purely conversational responses. I used the category "continue" for comparison. I did not want to include "other" because many mother responses categorized as "other" are teaching responses to the children's acts; they are not conversational. See Carol's mother's responses 2, 3, and 4; 7 and 8; and

15 and 16. The category "continue" includes mothers' verbalizations on topics about which the child has made an utterance but which do not include the word or words of the child's verbalization, positive feedback, or requests for clarification. "Continue" is conversational, not instructional. Table 7.5 presents the mothers' first and second responses to infant verbalizations at 18 and 24 months, grouped according to their teaching or conversational function. It can be seen by comparing teaching and "continue" percentages of first responses at 18 months that teaching responses are at least twice as great a percentage as "continue" responses for each mother. Teaching responses are a greater percentage of second responses for all mothers than "continue" at 18 months, although the percentages are much more variable.

Looking at the third column, first response after one-word utterance at 24 months, it can be seen that Carol's and Jean's mothers have reversed their pattern of response. For both mothers the percentage of "continue" responses is now at least twice as great as the percentage of teaching responses. This is not the case with Joel's and Allen's mothers. It should be remembered that Joel and Allen are not as advanced in their language development as Carol and Jean.

Looking at column 5, "first response after a multiword utterance," it can be seen that Carol's, Joel's, and Allen's mothers have higher percentages of teaching responses than "continue" responses (as expected) and that Joel's and Allen's mothers have more than twice as many. The exception is Jean's mother, whose style of interaction with Jean is primarily conversational when Jean is 24 months old. Table 7.5 provides some evidence that word teaching is elicited from mothers by their children's utterances. The proportion of

TABLE 7.5. Mother Responses to Infant Verbalizations

	1	2	3	4	5	6
	18 MONTHS		24 MONTHS			
	1st response following 1 word	2nd response following 1 word	1st 1 w	2nd 1 w	1st 2+ w	2nd 2+ w
PERCENTAGE RESPONSES 4, 5, 6, 7 OF TOTAL MOTHER RESPONSES						
Carol	74	61	27	33	53	22
Jean	68	36	21	18	25	14
Joel	50	30	53	0	57	42
Allen	53	23	43	59	59	25
PERCENTAGE CONTINUE						
Carol	11	17	55	33	41	78
Jean	21	24	71	50	40	78
Joel	7	13	29	64	21	33
Allen	21	20	43	25	24	50

4 = Says again
5 = Frames
6 = Positive feedback
7 = Request clarification

teaching after one-word utterances is in accord with the children's linguistic development. Mothers' first responses to multiword utterances at 24 months seem to be appropriate to the language learning task of generating multiword utterances, except for Jean's mother. She, unlike the other mothers, brings up for discussion such topics as tonight's dinner guests. What makes her unlike Carol's mother is her low percentage of teaching responses to multiword utterances (25 percent). She has a relatively high percentage of "change subject" responses (30 percent) where Carol's mother has 6 percent and Allen's and Joel's have zero. Jean's mother is not as likely to make a reinforcing, teaching response following a multiword utterance by Jean. She is much more likely than the other mothers to change the subject. (This research and these findings are more fully described in Holzman, 1983, unpublished.)

SYNTAX AT AGE TWO

At the beginning of this chapter I stated that it appears as though Allen, Carol, Jean, and Joel's early utterances were governed by discourse rules, and later discourse rules were supplanted by the syntactical rules of English. At age two all four children produce both topic-comment utterances and syntactically correct sentences. The majority (64 percent) of Carol's multi-word utterances were syntactically correct sentences; almost half (44 percent) of Jean's, 20 percent of Joel's and 23 percent of Allen's were. At the same time Carol produced the greatest number of different types of syntactically well-formed sentences, and Jean the second. (A list of the different types of sentences with examples is given in the appendix to this chapter.) In another two years or so, all of the children's speech will reflect their competence with the syntax of the English language. At two years varying proportions of their utterances are still governed by earliest rules, the discourse rules. Even so, I want to compare their language with that of the linguistic apes. I do this in order to judge whether the language behavior of the apes is sufficiently like that of children at two years that we would say that the apes are using a human language.

A SECOND LOOK AT LINGUISTIC APES

The characteristic that sets human language apart from animal signaling and even such elaborate serial conditioned behavior as that of Sarah, the linguistic ape described in Chapter Three, is that human language has syntactic rules. So any language behavior that we would characterize as being the same as that of human beings must have syntax. Roger Brown (1980) defines syntactic capacity as "the ability to put symbols (words) in construction so as to express compositional meanings which are other than the sum of the meanings of the individual symbols." In English, linear word order is a syntactic marker, and we recognize that "dog bites man" and "man bites dog" do not mean the same thing. The presence in utterances of complex hierarchical structures and grammatical morphemes are the two other grammatical markers in English, and they are more reliable as indicators that utterances have syntactic structure because a string of symbols (or words) may accidently be a syntactically correct NP, VP sentence. If the chimp, Nim, says, "Nim eat," that is an NP, VP sentence, but it may not have been constructed by Nim as such. He may simply have felt hunger pangs, pronounced his name and "eat," the idea that the hunger pang was associated with in his mind.

It is absence of one or more of the syntactic markers discussed in Chapter Six that makes the percentages of syntactically well-formed sentences produced by the children at two years less than 100 percent (see table 7.1).

In English linear word order is rule governed, and all the children's utterances deemed syntactically correct have English word order.

1. Joel: Sit down that way. (to mother to get her to move to another spot)
2. Carol: There's my other shoe.
3. Jean: I'm all done, 'kay?
4. Allen: I wanna watch.

Word order is the syntactic requirement that these children and the children studied by others (see Brown 1973, for example) master first. Grammatical morphemes that are syntactic requirements are very often missing in sentences with correct word order, as in the following: (Grammatical morphemes are underlined in (5) through (8).)

5. Carol: Joanna very pretty tak<u>ing a</u> picture.
6. Jean: I go<u>ing to</u> potty.
7. Allen: Happ<u>y</u> birthday finish.
8. Joel: Man fell down <u>dat</u> cup.

The following are the sentences with the missing grammatical markers supplied:

9. Joanna <u>is</u> very pretty taking a picture.
10. I <u>am</u> going to <u>the</u> potty.
11. <u>The</u> happy birthday <u>is</u> finish<u>ed</u>. ("Happy birthday" meant "birthday party" to Allen at two years and three weeks of age.)
12. <u>The</u> man fell down <u>from</u> dat cup.

In the early months of language use, grammatical morphemes are sometimes supplied by children and sometimes not. An interaction sequence for a 30-

month-old child shows the child including the contracted form *is* in some sentences, "Dat's green," and leaving it out in others, "Dat green," for no discernible reason (deVilliers and deVilliers 1980, p. 90). Roger Brown (1973) states that the 14 required grammatical markers that he investigated are not reliably present in children's speech until the child's MLU equals 4 morphemes. The age of children at MLU = 4 varies. The MLU of Carol, Jean, Allen, and Joel at two years ranges from 1.8 for Allen, Jean, and Joel to 2.5 for Carol, and the proportion of their speech that is syntactically correct ranges from 20 percent for Joel to 64 percent for Carol. These proportions meet the three syntactic criteria, one of which is presence of required grammatical morphemes.

Unfortunately we cannot use presence of grammatical morphemes in judging whether the linguistic apes, Nim and Washoe, have human language because the sign language they have been taught does not have grammatical mophemes (Terrace 1979).[2] Therefore, in comparing the language use of the linguistic apes to the children, we have only linear order and hierarchical structure on which to make comparisons.

What one notices about the utterances of children who are beginning language use is that their longer utterances convey more meaning than their shorter utterances. It is true, perhaps, that "milk" said in a plaintive voice by a one-year-old conveys the same information as "I want a glass of milk" said by a three-year-old. However, all the information is conveyed in words by the three-year-old and the information is more precise. This is one of the great powers of language as a means of communication. It can be used all by itself without its being necessary to hear the message spoken or see the speaker and the context in which the message was spoken. (It is this that makes written language and our consequent ability to store information in books possible.)

Comparisons of language behavior will be made with Nim because he is the only linguistic ape being taught sign language for whom sufficient data have been published to make a comparison (Terrace 1979).

The psychologists who have worked with other linguistic apes are Allen and Beatrice Gardner and Roger Fouts with Washoe, and Francine Patterson with Koko. It seems reasonable to use Nim as our prototypical linguistic ape because none of the other psychologists have published data concerning Washoe, Koko, or any other ape being taught sign language that differs from Terrace's (Brown 1980).

There is general agreement that apes can learn to associate a visual symbol, either a token (as was used with Sarah) or a sign (used with Nim and Washoe) with a referent like banana or tickle. In order to investigate whether there is evidence that these symbols are used in syntactic constructions or are simply strings or symbols associated with the ideas as they come to Nim's mind, we will look at Nim's four-sign combinations and compare them with

---

[2]In all cases a sign language called pidgin signed English, not ASL (American Sign Language), which is the usual sign language of the deaf in the United States, is the sign language taught to the linguistic apes.

the four-word combinations of Allen, Carol, Jean, and Joel. The reasons for making the comparison between four-word and four-sign combinations is that longer combinations are less likely than shorter combinations to be syntactically well formed "by coincidence" or because the combination has been learned by rote.

Four-Word Utterances of Children

Allen   *Preceding* utterance or event[++]

*13. Put him in, man.   Allen: put him in.
 14. I wanna watch.   (Allen looks at portapak)
 15. Happy birthday to you.   Mother: Do you remember when we said Happy Birthday to Allen?
 16. (later on the tape) Happy birthday to you.   (Allen has arranged his toy animals around a pretend table.)

Joel

*17. No water in eyes.   Mother: You're going to get water in your eyes.
*18. Joel lie down too.   (Joel has told mother to lie down and she has complied.)
*19. No water in it.   (Joel is looking at cup from which he has poured water.)
*20. No water down there.   (The water has drained out of the bath tub.)
*21. Water out there 'gain.
*22. No Joel's towel here.
 23. Sit down that way.   (showing his mother where to sit)
*24. No water out there.
 25. Carry it that way.

Jean

 26. Get more water, kay?
*27. No them not mine.
 28. I want 'nother one.
 29. No need a towel.
 29. I need a towel.
 30. I don't know.
 31. I want it now.
 32. Yeah, I make it.
*33. How come no bubbles.
*34. Over there no bubbles.
*35. I'm come out.

*Indicates that the utterance is not a grammatical sentence.

[++]Preceding utterance or event has been included where Allen's and Joel's utterances need some explanation.

36. Look at my bottle.
*37. Lie down, my bear.
38. Mommy's all wet.
39. I put more, 'kay.
40. I wan 'nother bottle.
41. I need water here.

Carol
*42. Come here get hammer
43. Where's the soap
*44. make it the rain
*45. hand in the box
*46. Put my head down
47. it doesn't work
*48. Ring went in there
49. Get the ring out
*50. My face all done
51. Put it up here
*52. Then went in car
53. Make this one fall
54. Here, look at this
55. This is happy birthday
*56. going put 'em here

Allen and Joel did not produce many four-word utterances at two years, three weeks but the ones they did produce had the word order of English sentences except for Allen's "put him in, man." This utterance is what I have called a topic-comment utterance, a presyntactic utterance. The well-formed version would be "put the man in." This is the only four-word utterance by any of the children that does not have English word order. Many of the utterances are not syntactically well formed because required grammatical morphemes have not been supplied. Since the sign equivalents of grammatical morphemes do not exist in the sign language being taught Nim, no comparison of their presence in the children's and in Nim's utterances is possible. Of the 21 most frequent four-sign combinations produced by Nim (see Table 7.6), I can find only one in which there are not repeated signs and in which the sequence of four signs conveys a unified message.

57. Me eat drink more

There are two combinations that have the structure of topic-comment utterances like Allen's "put him in, man."

58. banana, me eat banana
59. play me Nim play

TABLE 7.6. Most Frequent Four-Sign Combinations (Nim)

Four sign combinations	Frequency
eat drink eat drink	15
eat Nim eat Nim	7
banana Nim banana Nim	5
drink Nim drink Nim	5
banana eat me Nim	4
banana me eat Nim	4
banana me Nim me	4
grape eat Nim eat	4
Nim eat Nim eat	4
play me Nim play	4
drink eat drink eat	3
drink eat me Nim	3
eat grape eat Nim	3
eat me Nim drink	3
grape eat me Nim	3
me eat drink more	3
me eat me eat	3
me gum me gum	3
me Nim me eat	3
Nim me Nim me	3
tickle me Nim play	3

Terrace 1979

My attempts to find more order in this set of utterances as four-sign combinations failed because of (1) the lack of consistency in the order of the signs—for example, sometimes Nim signs "me eat" and sometimes "eat me"—and (2) the repetition of signs in a combination. Nine of the 21 combinations are of the form:

sign one	sign two	sign three	sign four
eat	drink	eat	drink
me	eat	me	eat

"Me eat drink more" could be verb coordination with *and* not supplied between the verbs.

There are no four-sign utterances for Nim that are compelling evidence of hierarchical organization in Nim's combinations, but this may be a function of his never having been exposed to hierarchical organization of sign combinations. Complex structures of the children's in which hierarchical organization can be seen are

Carol
Come here get hammer

Make it the rain
Make this one fall

and the verb complement utterances with *wanna* produced by the other children. In addition to the evidence that Nim's four-sign combinations are strings rather than syntactic constructions, both Terrace and Brown cite two other findings that provide evidence that ape symbolic behavior is not like the language behavior of young children. The MLU of child speech or child signing (the language behavior of deaf children) rises steadily with age for all children for several years. This is not the case for Nim, whose MLU (in signs) fluctuated erratically between 1.1 and 1.6 between the ages of 26 and 45 months. (None of the other psychologists have published MLU data for apes differing from Terrace's.)

Finally, the language behavior of children is, for the most part, spontaneous and, once children are beyond the one-word stage, it is a natural part of their interaction with family members and caregivers. This does not seem to be the case with the linguistic apes. Terrace reports that prompting by the psychologist plays a major role in generating signing behavior from the ape. (This can be seen in the films the Gardners have made with Washoe.) It is like the verbal interactions in the one-word period when mother says, "What does the kitty say?" and baby says, "meow," or when a great many of some infant's utterances *are* imitations of the last word of mother's utterances. Joel was such an infant.

For now, it continues to look as though human language, with its syntactic component, is uniquely human.

HUMAN BEINGS WITHOUT SYNTACTIC LANGUAGE

Most human beings have syntactic language. Who are the ones who do not? There are some human beings so profoundly retarded in their mental development that they, literally, cannot do anything for themselves, including walking and talking. There are *aphasic* human beings, persons of normal intellectual endowment who have an abnormality or injury that affects the areas of the brain specialized to language and speech functions and whose abilities to understand and/or produce linguistic speech are impaired.

There are also a few cases of children who have grown past puberty outside of human society. The best documented case is that of Victor, the wild boy of Aveyron who was captured in the woods near Aveyron in southern France in 1798 (Itard 1962).

Victor came under the care of Dr. J. Itard, a humane physician who tried to teach language to Victor. Victor learned words and learned to use them to make requests. Despite years of loving care and instruction, Victor never acquired syntactic language. However, all this took place almost two centuries ago, and what was learned about Victor is limited because of the lack of understanding of language and brain function at that time. We still do not have anything like full understanding, but we are more knowledgable now than then. And, unfortunately, there is Genie to study, a young person isolated and confined to a small room from the age of 20 months until she was 13 years and 7 months old. At that time she was taken into protective custody by the police and brought to Children's Hospital, Los Angeles. Genie was hospitalized for severe malnutrition. At the time she was not toilet trained and could not stand erect or chew food. She produced no vocal sounds. She had been placed under increasing physical restraint over the years, spending most of her time harnessed to an infant potty. Genie was given minimal care by a mother who was going blind. Genie was physically punished by her father if she made a noise. He father could not stand any noise. There was no television or radio in the house. It is known that her father and older brother did not speak to her but rather barked at her like dogs. For the most part she was alone and under restraint for almost 13 years. The extent of the language spoken to Genie during this time is not known. It is assumed to have been minimal.

In the year following her discovery Genie went to live with a foster family but continued to receive care, instruction, and evaluation from the hospital and particularly from Dr. Susan Curtis of UCLA, who has worked with Genie since she was found in 1970. Dr. Curtis wrote that, although Genie has developed a large vocabulary and speaks multiword utterances, Genie's speech is "telegrammatic and lacks all of the morphological and syntactic devices for unambiguously marking grammatical relations" (Curtis 1980, p. 9). Genie lacks a syntactic grammar even though she is an intelligent young person as measured by performance on tests of cognitive development.

According to Curtis, Genie's language development is like that of deaf persons who have not been exposed to a syntactic sign language until after puberty; it is like that of children who have had the left hemisphere of their brains removed. In all these cases language is learned with the right hemisphere of the brain and the individual fails to develop a syntactic grammar. Curtis (1980), and many others, explain these facts in the following way:

1. Language is primarily lateralized to the left hemisphere of the brain (as described in Chapter Six).
2. There is a critical period for acquisition of language with the left hemisphere which ends at puberty.
3. Some aspects of language are acquirable in both the left and right hemispheres, but not syntax.

Genie, who received only minimal exposure to language before puberty, and the deaf persons, not exposed to a syntactic sign language until after puberty, learn language with their right hemisphere because the critical period for language learning with the left hemisphere has passed. Language learned with the right hemisphere does not have a syntactic grammar because syntax is a left hemisphere function.

Children who have had their left hemispheres removed also have only their right hemispheres with which to acquire language. They have essentially normal intelligence but lack syntactic language.

Syntactic language is the uniquely human language. How human beings come to have it is still not well understood. No one has yet given us an explanation of the relation between language and the brain that is generally accepted in its entirety.

Appendix:
Types of the Children's
Syntactically Well-Formed Sentences
at Age Two[3]

The types of the children's syntactically well-formed utterances and examples of each type are:

1. SP, a sentence composed of an NP and VP where NP is the subject and VP the predicate of the sentence.

1. Jean: I wan 'nother bottle.
2. Joel: Mommy do it.
3. Allen: Here it is.

2. SPQ, an interrogative, subject predicate sentence.

4. Carol: whatcha doing?
5. Jean: I put more, kay?
6. Joan: I'm all done, kay?

---

[3]The "types" are those identified in the coding system used. The coding system did not identify negative utterances. These are simply included in the appropriate category. The coding system does not distinguish *wh* questions, yes/no, and tag questions. The decision to categorize in this way was made to avoid proliferation of categories that were not of special interest in the research.

Jean formed yes/no interrogatives at age two by adding an interrogative tag: ok? At this age only Carol and Jean produced well-formed questions. Carol's well-formed questions (or interrogatives) included *wh* questions, questions which start with *when, what, who,* or *where.*

   7. Carol: Where's the soap?

   3. SPcmp, a complex subject predicate sentence.

   8. Carol: wanna hit the pink one?

Although (8) would not be considered well formed in isolation, it is all right in a two-person, face-to-face conversation where speech is informal. The *do* that begins the question in formal speech can be left out, as can the subject pronoun, because it will be clear from the context who the understood subject is.

   9. Allen: I wanna watch.
  10. Joel: wanna get out.

In (10), the subject pronoun *I* is lacking, but is acceptable in two-person, face-to-face conversation.

   4. SP ellipsis, linguistic ellipsis. The syntactically well-formed sentence can be constructed from the ellipsis and the previous sentence in the discourse using the rules of English grammar.

  11. Carol: I can't.
  12. Carol: I do.

Only Carol has learned to make an ellipsis of a verb phrase in the preceding utterance by using first auxiliaries like *can't* and *do* but Jean (and maybe Joel) produces utterances that supply a syntactically correct phrase for a preceding mother utterance like (13), (14), (15), and (16).

Mother	*Jean*
What are we going to do with this?	13. Drink it.
Where'd the water go?	14. Down dere.
Where shall we put them?	15. with mine.
Where shall we put it while you take your bath?	16. In there.

Mother asked Joel, "What were you dressed up as on Halloween?" Joel has misunderstood and answered, "Trick or treat?" Then, Mother rephrased her question.

| Mother: What kind of mask did you have? | 17. Joel: Kitten mask. |

Jean produced a sufficient number of different phrases to credit her with the ability to supply a syntactically correct phrase for a preceding mother sentence. Joel produced only (17), and although Allen responded to mother utterances, none of his responses were linguistic ellipses.

5. P, syntactically well-formed sentences that do not have a subject NP in their constituent structure.

Carol
18. Taste that.
19. Hit the purple one.
20. Open the door.
21. Turn the water.
22. Wash my hand.

Joel
23. Sit down.
24. Lie down.
25. Sleep tight.
26. Cut it.
27. Carry it that way.

Jean
28. Make soup.
29. Take it.
30. Hold it.
31. Look at my bottle.

Allen
32. Turn over.
33. Open it.
34. Hide it.
35. Drink it.

6. Pcmp, complex predicate sentences.

36. Carol: Make this one fall.
37. Carol: Let's put them together again.

7. Coordination.

38. Jean: That's Mommy's and Daddy's.
39. Jean: Take Mommy's and then don't touch Daddy's, kay?

Only Carol produced complex predicate sentences and only (36) and (37).

Only Jean produced any instances of coordination in her sentences, and (38) and (39) are the only instances.

The distribution of syntactically well-formed sentences of these four children shows that the largest number of such sentences for all children are SP and P sentences. Carol, Joel, and Allen produced predicate complement sentences with *wanna* (want to). These are complex (SPcmp) sentences. Carol produced all the types of syntactically well-formed sentences identified by the coding system except compound sentences and Jean, all except PCMP, complex predicate sentences.

8

The Communication Skills of Young Children

If you heard the question,

1. "Did li'l tweetie faw down?"

being asked in a tender, rather high pitched voice, you wouldn't have much trouble figuring out who was being asked if he or she had fallen down. It would most likely be a very young child because this question is being asked in the *baby talk register* of American English. All languages have several registers, different sets of rules for using the language depending upon who is talking to whom and whether the language is being used for talking or writing. In Chapter Twelve, we will discuss rules for language use depending on the sex, social status, and age of the talkers; in this chapter we will discuss baby talk and more generally the communication skills of young children.

THE BABY TALK REGISTER

The features of the baby talk register include speaking in short utterances, a good deal of repetition of utterances, and speaking at a higher than usual pitch with exaggerated intonation. Speaking more slowly and clearly than usual are sometimes baby talk register characteristics. Simplifying the pronunciation of words as in *li'l* for *little, tweetie* for *sweetie,* and *faw* for *fall* is probably less frequently a feature than the others, in part at least, because we have been taught that doing this interferes with young children's learning to pronounce the words correctly. They will try to pronounce what they hear.

The features just mentioned do not exhaust the list that has been proposed for the baby talk register. There is no hard and fast list of features, but there is a short list of the ways in which the features of the register make it a better means of communication with very young children than the adult register. Ferguson (1977) lists simplifying, clarifying, and expressive as the characteristics of the register, which its special features foster. Short utterances are generally simpler than longer ones and easier for the young child to understand and produce. Repetition of utterances clarifies them because, in the first place, the repetition provides further opportunity for the infant to hear, remember, and figure out what the verbalization means and what its structure is. Speaking extra slowly and clearly also enhances the child's chances of being able to figure out the meaning and structure of the verbalization. The adult's pronouncing *little* as *li'l* serves no purpose. The young child sometimes has difficulty pronouncing some speech sounds, particularly consonant clusters like the *tl* cluster in *little,* and simplifies in his or her own pronunciation. The child's problem is in articulating the sounds, not in hearing them, and the adult who adopts a babyish pronunciation of words is simply misinforming the infant language learner. Perhaps the unconscious motivation for babyish pronunciation is the expressive characteristic of the register. The adult is expressing tenderness and the feeling that the infant should be responded to in a special way. Use of higher than usual pitch and exaggerated intonation are motivated by the adult expressive purpose. These features capture and keep the baby's interest in what the speaker is saying. The speech of the mothers of Allen, Carol, Jean, and Joel to their infants displayed the baby talk register features discussed except for simplified pronunciation.

I have not yet mentioned another commonly suggested feature of the baby talk register: using *mommy* and *Allen,* for example, in face-to-face discourse where, if adults were talking to each other, they would use the personal pronouns, *you, I, me, yours,* and *mine.* The reason suggested for using *mommy* and the child's name instead of the pronouns is that the child doesn't have to shift from second to first person to answer his mother's questions.

2. Do you want a cookie?
3. I do.
4. Does Joel want a cookie?
5. Joel does.

It is assumed that (4) and (5) are "easier" than (2) and (3) because (4) and (5) do not necessitate a pronoun shift. Our findings suggest something else. We put all the utterances of the mothers of Allen, Carol, Jean, and Joel when the infants were 3, 6, 9, and 12 months old into the computer and got a rank order for the frequency of words spoken for each mother. We found that, at all data points, *you* was among the three most frequent words, *I* was among the top ten and *mommy* or *mother* were not spoken at all. When Allen was 12 months old, *Allen* was among his mother's top ten words, but *Allen* was used to get his attention, not as a subject or object in sentences. It was not that these mothers were not using the baby talk register, for they were. The average length of their verbalizations to their infants was between three and four words at every data point and all four engaged in much repetition of utterances. Their speech was marked by exaggerated intonation; in addition to the use of higher than usual pitch, they sometimes whispered and growled. When the children were well into the one-word period, there were scattered instances of the use of *mommy* and infant's name as sentence constituents. But they tended to follow the child's use of mommy or his own name. Joel said *mommy* holding a book out toward his mother. Joel's mother said,

6. You want Mommy to read it?

Joel's mother used the word *mommy* because Joel had just used it, and she expanded Joel's utterance into a sentence. Her question provided a little lesson for Joel about how to put his request in "better" English, and at the same time her question acted as a check on their communication. She was asking Joel if by *mommy* and the gesture of handing over the book, he meant he wanted her to read it. She could have said, "You want me to read it?" and not repeated Joel's *mommy*. I think that mothers' repetition of their infants' words in the one-word period serves a word-teaching function. I am not sure how conscious mothers (and others) are that they are adapting their speech so that it is comprehensible to their children and is providing language lessons. Cross (1977) has produced evidence that mothers speech to children between the ages of 19 and 32 months is "finely tuned" to the psycholinguistic capabilities of the children. What that means is that there are highly significant differences in mothers' speech to children in this restricted age range that depend on the capacities of the children rather than their ages. Cross concludes that mother speech to children is adapted, in a finely tuned way, to the rapidly changing psycholinguistic capacities of young children. I very much doubt whether mothers have the finely tuned adaption of their speech to the rapidly changing capacities of their children under their voluntary or conscious control. The ability to adapt language use to the needs of the developing language user appears to be an aspect of the innate, linguistic capacity of the human species, like the vocalizing and word-teaching behaviors of mothers described in Chapters Four and Seven.

THE SOCIOLINGUISTIC SKILLS OF PRESCHOOL CHILDREN

Research that suggests an innate predisposition of humans to adapt language use concerns the ability of four-year-old boys, with no younger brothers or sisters, to adapt their language use to low verbal (MLUs 1.0-1.5) as opposed to high verbal (MLUs 1.8-4.0) two-year-olds. The two-year-old groups did not differ in age, cognitive ability, or maturity of their behavior, so what the four-year-olds were responding to was just the difference in the linguistic performance of the two-year-olds. The researcher, Elise Masur, had ten four-year-old boys each explain to one high verbal and one low verbal two-year-old boy how to play with a toy filling station with a ramp, an elevator, and a garage. The four-year-olds explained the filling station to one of the two-year-olds on one day and the other on another day. Five of the four-year-olds explained the toy to his high verbal two-year-old first and the other five explained first to the low verbal two-year-old. Masur computed the mean length of utterance for the four-year-old boys on their first ten verbalizations to the two-year-old boys. She has reported (Masur 1978) that the MLUs of the four-year-old boys were significantly higher to the high verbal two-year-olds than to the low verbal two-year-olds, except to the five low verbal two-year-olds who did not speak at all. When the two-year-olds did not speak, the MLUs of the four-year-olds were like those to the high verbal two-year-olds. These results show that people as young as four years of age have the capacity to adapt their speech to the capacity of the listener as revealed by the listener's MLU. If the listener didn't speak, then the clue to his psycholinguistic capacity was lacking, and the speaker did not adjust his speech.

Masur calculated MLUs on the first ten utterances rather than on the utterances of the entire session because, as the two-year-olds began to manipulate the filling station and the cars, short utterances predominated for both the four-year-olds and two-year-olds. Their talk was mostly in direct response to each other, checking and clarifying what should be done with the toy. "This way?" was said by a two-year-old as he placed a car on the ramp. "Okay," responded the four-year-old.

Masur's findings are important because mothers' fine tuning of their speech to their own infants is one thing, but four-year-old boys with no younger siblings fine tuning *their* speech to two-year-olds they have just met is quite another. Arguments that seem plausible about implications of adults' experience and cognitive development in their adapting to their infants are not so plausible with four-year-old boys. It seems more likely that the ability of human beings, even as young as four years of age, to adapt their speech to the psycholinguistic capacity of very young children is part of our innate linguistic endowment rather than something learned through experience.

EGOCENTRISM AND PERSPECTIVE-TAKING

Psycholinguists who believe that adaptation of one's speech to the needs of a beginning language user is learned through experience would argue that each person's experiences as a beginning language provides the experience necessary to be able to adapt speech to other beginning language users; in other words, any human being who has become a language user has been through the beginning language user experience and therefore is able to take the perspective of the beginning language user. However, it has been widely assumed by psychologists that perspective-taking is a cognitive skill that does not develop in the human being until the person is about seven years of age. Before this human beings are not aware that other people may have perspectives that are different from their own. This is what is meant by egocentrism. This is the theory of Jean Piaget, and it has dominated cognitive developmental psychology since the 1960s. The finding that four-year-old boys vary their speech to high verbal and low verbal two-year-olds would be difficult for Piaget's theory to explain, even if the onset of the ability to take the perspective of another were moved down to four years, because a person could not have been both a high verbal and low verbal two-year-old.

Most of the studies of communication that have been done using young children as subjects have found that they are poor communicators, and very often poor communication has been attributed to the lack of ability on the part of the sender of a message to take the perspective of the message receiver into account. The sender does not take into account what information the receiver needs.

REFERENTIAL COMMUNICATION

One of the types of communication between children that has been studied is referential communication. If one child can see an object hidden from the view of the second child, how do they communicate so that the second child finds out what the object is that the first child sees? A common way to investigate the problem is to seat the children facing each other at a table with a barrier between them so that they cannot see each other or the other's side of the table. The object (usually a picture of an object) to be communicated is placed on the table in front of the child who is designated the speaker, and the speaker describes the object for the listener who cannot see it. On the basis of the speaker's description, feedback from the listener (if there is any), and the speaker's responses to the listener's feedback (if there are any and the interchange goes on as long as speaker and listener continue), the listener decides what the object is. Obviously, this can be so easy that there is no communication problem. If the picture is of a familiar object, such as a dog, a candy cane, or a horse, the task is so easy that nothing can be learned about communication. Research has been concerned with discovering how communication is accomplished when it is difficult. Over the course of many experiments we have come to see that being unable to take the perspective of another may not be the only reason, and may not be the reason at all, why communication fails. I have just said that it would be easy for one child to communicate the subject of a picture to another if the picture were of a dog or a candy cane, and this is because the object is a familiar one and has a name known to all. The referential communication task usually involves communicating the identity of one of several objects in the picture that are difficult to distinguish or which do not have names.

The following paragraphs describe one such experiment.

The listeners have a page before them on their side of the barrier like Figure 8.1. Half of the speakers in this experiment (Carrier and Leet, 1972) have a page just like Figure 8.1 except that the middle line with the half-circle has a gold star pasted under it to indicate to the speaker that this is the target drawing that he or she is supposed to identify for the listener. The other half of the speakers have a page before them that has only the middle line with the half-circle on it. Having speakers who can see exactly what information the listeners have (speakers who have all three drawings on their pages) and speakers who have only the target drawing permits the experimenter to test whether knowing exactly how things look from the listener's perspective improves communication. When there are a small number of alternatives side by side, as in Figure 8.1, and the speakers have the same page as the listeners, they can identify the target for the listeners by saying, "It's the middle one." The second graders in this experiment who had pages just like the listeners for the 11 different targets rarely used position to identify the target drawing. Typically, speakers described the drawings as objects as much as possible. One speaker whose page had only the target drawing on it described it successfully to his listener: "It's half a ball going up." Another successful pair with a speaker who had all three drawings had a listener (Petie) who consistently took the initiative and described the pictures as objects.

> Petie: Is it shaped like a devil's fork for one thing?
> Cyrus: No.
> Petie: Is it shaped like an arrow?

FIGURE 8.1. Line with half-circle figures from Carrier-Leet experiment (1972).

Cyrus: No.
Petie: OK, I got it.

What impressed Carrier and Leet about the children's performance on this referential communication task was that they did not see the task the same way the researchers did. Carrier and Leet expected the children to have a serious task oriented attitude. The children tended to treat the task as a guessing game, which they enjoyed and wanted to prolong, so speakers sometimes gave "hints" rather than adequate information. This can be seen in the exchange between Maria (speaker) and Carol (listener) on the target shown in Figure 8.2. Maria (speaker) had only the target drawing, the set of dots on the left, on her page.

Maria: It's black.
Carol: I have plenty of black things here.
Maria: (Silence)
Carol: If I was on that side I couldn't think of anything to say either.
Maria: If I tell her the thing I'm thinking of, she'll probably know it. (Said to experimenter)
Maria: Four dots.
Carol: They all have four dots.
Maria: They're black and first it goes up and then comes back down and stays some more.

Carrier and Leet found that their subjects' ambiguous and egocentric responses were most frequent on the difficult trials, like Figure 8.2. Here is the interchange between Michele and Munchie, a pair with a speaker (Michele) who had all three drawings of Figure 8.2 on her page.

Michele: It's left. (Michele is identifying the target drawing by its position on the page.)
Munchie: My left or your left?
Michele: I don't know. Over there (pointing).
Experimenter: Try to use words.
Michele: It's on the side close to Maria's mother.
Munchie: That's my right.
Michele: No, it's left.
Munchie: It's my right.
Michele: Tough luck.

FIGURE 8.2*. Dot figures from Carrier-Leet experiment (1972). (*Maria's page had only the drawing on the left, the target drawing.)

Michele and Munchie's problem arose, not because Michele initially failed to take Munchie's perspective but because right and left are cognitively difficult. Munchie knew that people facing each other have their right and left sides opposite each other. She did not know that her question was just going to confuse Michele because the relationship between target and side of the page is independent of Michele's and her position vis-à-vis each other. The target was on the left side of the page for both girls. This is not a problem caused by the failure to realize that there is another perspective other than one's own. Michele's and Munchie's communication about the target broke down because of cognitive overload. Neither understood the problem of coordinating their perspectives and their pages. Research has shown that even four- and five-year-olds are capable of taking the perspective of another if the communication task is cognitively simple. Maratsos (1973), for example, found that four- and five-year-olds understood that a blindfolded person needed information that a sighted person did not.

ROLE-TAKING

An elegant demonstration that cognitive complexity rather than lack of ability to take another's perspective caused failure on a role-taking task has been made by M. Shatz (1978). Her subjects were four- and five-year-olds. She showed each of them a picture of a child who was either the same age as the subject or was a two-year-old and asked the subject to pick a present for the child from a group of four toys. Two of the four toys, a pull toy and a set of stacking toys, would be appropriate for a two-year-old; two toys, a magnetic board with letters and numbers and a set of sewing cards, would be appropriate for a preschooler like the subject. Then subjects were invited to pick out a toy for themselves. Shatz's results are shown in Tables 8.1 and 8.2.

Table 8.1 shows that only ten of the 58 subjects chose a toy that was not appropriate for the intended recipient, the child whose picture Shatz had shown them. Table 8.2 shows that subjects were unlikely to pick for themselves the same toy as they had picked for a two-year-old. Only five of 29 subjects did so, showing that, when they picked a toy for a two-year-old, it was not on the basis of their own preferences.

Shatz then made her task more difficult by adding two more toys: a teething ring and a rattle appropriate for a baby, or an activity-puzzle book

TABLE 8.1. Preschoolers Selecting a Given Type Toy, Four-Toy Experiment (N = 58)

	TOYS APPROPRIATE FOR	
Intended recipient	Two-year-olds	Preschoolers
Two-year-old	21	8
Preschooler	2	27

Shatz 1978

TABLE 8.2. Subjects Picking Same or Different Toy for Self, Four-Toy Experiment

	TOYS FOR SELF	
Intended recipient	Different	Same as for other
Two-year-old	24	5
Preschooler	17	12

Shatz 1978

and a game called Racko appropriate for a school-age child. This time the task was the same for all subjects: select a toy for a two-year-old child. It was more difficult than before because there were *six* toys appropriate to *three* ages from which to choose rather than *four* toys appropriate to *two* ages. Table 8.3 and 8.4 show the results when the added toys were for a school-age child or for a baby. If you compare Table 8.1 and 8.3, you can see that adding the two extra toys confused preschoolers. Even though only one preschooler picked a toy appropriate for a school-age child to give to a two-year-old, half the preschoolers picked a toy for a preschooler to give to the two-year-old (Table 8.3). When the preschoolers had only four toys to choose from, over two and a half times as many picked an appropriate toy as an inappropriate one (Table 8.1.). When the added toys were appropriate for an infant, toys for two-year-olds, preschoolers, and infants were picked almost equally often (Table 8.4).

What we can see from Shatz's experiment is that a task that preschoolers *can* do can be made so difficult by adding items to it that preschoolers can no longer do the task, even though it is the same task; this is because of cognitive overload. You can probably multiply 45 by 11 in your head but not 4932 by 673. They are both multiplication problems, but multiplying a four digit number by a three digit number entails remembering so many numbers, if you do it in your head, that it may not be possible to do the multiplication—a failure caused by cognitive overload, not by a failure to understand how to multiply.

Experimental work that caused people to conclude that preschoolers' communication fails because they are unable to take another's perspective may have been too difficult for preschoolers because of cognitive overload. When children do fail in a task, like Munchie and Michele, for example, they sometimes resort to quite immature tactics. Possibly they are responding to feelings of frustration. Have you ever seen an adult kick a door when a key wouldn't unlock it?

TABLE 8.3. Toy Selection for a Two-Year-Old with Added Toys for a School-Age Child

	TOYS APPROPRIATE FOR		
Age of subjects	Two-year-olds	Preschoolers	School-age
Four-year-olds	3	8	1
Five-year-olds	8	4	0
Total	11	12	1

Shatz 1978

TABLE 8.4. Toy Selection for a Two-Year-Old with Added Toys for an Infant

	TOYS APPROPRIATE FOR		
Age of subjects	Two-year-olds	Preschoolers	Infant
Four-year-olds	3	5	4
Five-year-olds	6	3	3
Total	9	8	7

Shatz 1978

9

Semantic Development

I have discussed the fact that young children just beginning to be language users are learning, primarily, the names of the interesting objects, activities, and qualities (like hot and cold) that are part of their experience and learning what their mothers (or other important persons) mean by their utterances. Children are associating linguistic entities with aspects of reality. We have seen that children learn, or acquire, the basics of the syntactic organization of their language very early.

In addition to being organized syntactically, language is semantically organized in the minds of its speakers, and this organization involves both language and thought. The evidence at this time is that syntactic organization, on the other hand, is independent of other cognitive systems. It has been pointed out by Vygotsky (1962) that there can be thought without language and language without thought. All the thought processes of the prelinguistic infant are thoughts without language. Piaget's theory is that prelinguistic infants think by acting on objects that they see, hear, and feel. There is language without thought whenever language is used ritualistically or in play without the words used having meaning for the user. Joel's game with his mother at 12 months of pointing and saying "kitty" is an example of language without thought. When the child begins to use words meaningfully, the semantic development of language begins. In the early years semantic development is mainly a matter of establishing relations between language spoken to or by the child and the experience the language glosses (matches, explains, or provides a running commentary for). By the time children are about five years old, there begin to be relations established in the child's mind between words, as well as between language and experience of the world. Semantic organization refers to the relations established between

115

words. Semantic organization of language has been studied in various ways, a few that relate to development of language in children will now be discussed.

WORD ASSOCIATIONS: THEIR DEVELOPMENT IN NORTH AMERICANS AND JAPANESE

One kind of semantic organization in the human mind can be observed by finding out which words are closely related so that thinking of one word reminds a person of another. When you read the word *apple*, what word comes to mind? For me, it is *orange*. Louis Moran (1973) did a study in which he compared the word associations of Japanese and North American preschool children and adults. He defined four different types of associations to classify the responses of his subjects to the 60 words he used as stimuli.

1. Functional—the association is between two physical referents (physical objects) used together.

Stimulus	*Response*
table	chair

2. Iconic—ascribes a quality to a referent.

Stimulus	*Response*
apple	red
brave	eagle

3. Enactive—action on referent.

Stimulus	*Response*
apple	eat
rip	pants

4. Logical—abstract relation between referents.

Stimulus	*Response*
table	furniture
strong	weak

For (4) *table* is a member of the superordinate class, *furniture,* and *strong* and *weak* are adjectives with the opposite meaning.

Moran's instruction was to say the first word that comes to mind when you hear each of the words on his list of 60. He found that both the Japanese and North American children gave primarily enactive responses. Japanese adults gave primarily iconic responses; 65 percent of North American adults' responses were logical and another 20 percent were functional.

Moran's findings suggest that preschoolers' semantic organization of language is similar for Japanese and North Americans. The great difference between the two adult populations suggests that culture, including schooling, plays a large part in determining the semantic organization of language in adults. In my seminar on language and thought we speculated that, if we tested college students who were (1) art, music, and literature majors and compared them to (2) science majors, we would find a difference like that between Japanese and North Americans. When we repeated Moran's experiment with the two groups, we were disappointed to find that the responses of both groups were primarily what Moran called logical. We had thought that having artistic temperments would cause art, music, and literature majors to have word associations that were more like those of the adult Japanese than the adult North Americans. We concluded that the influence of culture and schooling prevailed over possible artistic associations of the art, music, and literature majors.

Moran's adult North American responses and our experiment indicate that the most accessible semantic organization of language for English speaking North American adults is an abstract organization in which words are related to other words rather than to experience.

WAYS TO ORGANIZE
THE CONTENTS OF THE MIND

The enactive responses of the young children derive from their day-to-day experiences. Other investigators (such as Anglin 1977, Schlesinger, undated Mimeo) and I have proposed that the earliest concepts that children have for words are just memories of instances in which a word has been linked to a specific referent object, event, or experience. If one asks a young child what a dog is, the child will respond by telling an instance of personal experience with a dog associated in his memory with the word, *dog*.

After a number of encounters with dogs, the separate memories will coalesce to form an average or prototypical image in the child's memory. The prototypical image develops before the scientific analytical concept. The analytical concept is associated with *awareness* of both similarities and differences; the prototypical image with *lack of attention* to differences. An important difference between the two is that the prototypical image is the result of automatic, effortless mental processing while the analytical concept is the result of purposeful, deliberate mental processing. One implication of this difference is that, from an early age, everyone will have verbal concepts, information including names, for prototypical images. Anglin (1977) found that American preschool children identified pictures of unfamiliar species (such as the wombat, an Australian marsupial that resembles a bear) as animal while refusing to identify a picture of a familiar butterfly as animal; it was not the right shape. Anglin's subjects had a verbal concept, the word *animal,* for four legged furry creatures that looked like their mental image, their prototype.

An analytical concept is based on analysis of the attributes that are necessary for a particular object, like "dog" to be classified in a given category, like "mammal," and this is what makes the analytical concept purposeful and deliberate. Before they go to school, children are not likely to have analytical concepts for organizing the contents of their minds while adults and older children will. While it does not happen automatically, nevertheless a great deal of the work to organize language and thought in terms of analytic concepts is done in school.

I want to discuss prototypical mental images and analytical concepts as ways of organizing contents of the mind having to do with animals, and I know such discussions are easier with examples to think about. However, I do not want to present a prototypical image for mammal that seems to be the category Anglin's subjects thought of as animal. Just imagine the side view of an average size, four-footed, furry, nondescript animal and it will do. When a young child is asked whether a picture is an animal, as in Anglin's (1977) research, the child compares the picture with the prototypical mental image held in memory and decides. When an older child, who has been to school, is asked such a question by an experimenter, the older child responds differently. The typical concept formation experiment seems like school to a child, and he or she treats the question as if it were a question from teacher. (The typical experiment is probably being carried out in the school the child attends.) Science instruction begins in the first year of school, and children learn to distinguish fish, birds, and mammals in a scientific way—in terms of features rather than shapes. At the same time they learn that all three are examples of the superordinate concept, "animal" (see Table 9.1), and have features in common such as mobility and use of oxygen, which distinguish animal from the superordinate plant; plants use carbon dioxide and cannot move themselves.

Human beings have wonderfully complex filing systems for the contents of their minds. Being able to organize and store in memory the same content as analytic concepts based on defining features, as prototypical mental images, or just as the memories of an instance of experience are all three capacities of the adult and older child. Which method of organizing will be utilized at any time depends on the circumstances. I want to apply this analysis to preschool children's comprehension of spatial prepositions.

TABLE 9.1. The Superordinates *Animal* and *Plant* and the Analytic Concepts for Mammals, Fish, and Bird

SUPERORDINATE		ANIMAL			PLANT[a]

Features	Mammal	Fish	Bird	Others	Any plant
number of legs	4	none	2	?	No
wings	no	no	yes	?	No
live birth	yes	no	no	?	No
fur	yes	no	no	?	No
teeth	yes	yes	no	?	No
lungs	yes	no	yes	?	No
oxygen utilizing	yes	yes	yes	yes	No
mobile	yes	yes	yes	yes	No

[a]Plants have none of the listed features, which are defining or criterial features, of one or more of the animals (mammal, fish, bird).

PRESCHOOL CHILDREN'S COMPREHENSION OF SPATIAL PREPOSITIONS

I became interested in spatial prepositions because they are relational words. The nouns that children learn name objects or substances that have physical reality. Verbs do not name any thing, but the verbs children learn name physical activities, for the most part. Verbs need a subject so that a mental image can be evoked. The word *jump* all by itself does not name anything that can be visualized, but "Daddy jump" or "doggie jump" creates an image. Spatial prepositions are like verbs in that they cannot create an image standing alone. They differ from some verbs, like *jump,* which are exciting or interesting. The only motivation for learning the meanings of spatial prepositions is to clarify and refine sentence meaning.

As a first look at preschool children's understanding of spatial prepositions, my students and I did a comprehension experiment to see if preschool children understood the words *on, next to, in, underneath, behind, over, outside of, below, between, in front of, above, beside, inside, under* and *out of* (Holzman, 1981). Comprehension was tested in the context of a game in which the child placed a Cookie Monster doll in locations which were the referents of the prepositions. For the first experiment, child and experimenter sat next to each other facing the structure (see Figure 9.1). The first direction to the child was, "Put Cookie Monster *in* the red box"; the box was sitting on and glued to the middle shelf of the structure which was colored blue. Children were asked to respond to the prepositions in the order in which I have listed them. The majority of the children were able to respond correctly to all the prepositions. The errors made by the other children were heavily concentrated. At least 20 percent of the 70 children who participated in the experiment made errors on *underneath, below, over,* and *under.* I attribute the errors to these children's not having featural abstractions for the prepositions but, instead, having concepts for the prepositions that are mental images, coalescences of their memories of instances in their experience when the prepositions were used. Clues to the form of the mental images for *under* and *underneath* came from children who, when asked by the experimenter to put Cookie Monster under or underneath the red box, said, "I can't," or "it's stuck" (the red box glued to the shelf), or "He'll get squished" (Cookie Monster). These comments suggest that, for these children, *under* or *underneath* lies between the upper surface of the middle shelf and the bottom of the red box.

If you look at Figure 9.1, you can see that, in the structure for the first experiment, there was only one correct location, 6, to put Cookie Monster when the experimenter asked the child to put Cookie Monster under or underneath or below the red box. To be successful the child had to have an analytic featural concept for each of the prepositions so that location 6 would be seen to be correct. That is, the child had to see that location 6 was the only location available in the structure which had the necessary locational feature, situated lower than the reference object (the red box). The comments of the children, like the ones quoted previously, suggested that, if locations more like those designated "under" and "underneath" in the child's ordinary

FIGURE 9.1. Structure for comprehension experiment. (Figures from the Carrier-Leet experiment on referential communication.)

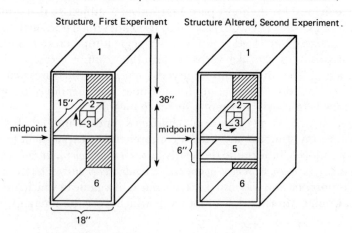

Structure, First Experiment   Structure Altered, Second Experiment.

experience were provided, errors on these two prepositions would be reduced. Furthermore, the location *in* was the incorrect response made 40 percent of the time when an error was made on *under, underneath,* or *below.* Since the red box was glued to the middle shelf, "in" is the location (3, on Figure 9.1) under the top of the red box. If children are accustomed to the locations "under the table," "under the chair," or "under the bed," the child's concept (mental image) would correspond to location 3 provided the child ignored the bottom of the box glued to the middle shelf.

We carried out a second experiment with the children to check this reasoning. For the second experiment we altered the blue structure (see Figure 9.1, altered structure) by ungluing the red box, providing location 4 so that children could put Cookie Monster on the middle shelf and hold the red box on or over his head. We also added a new shelf just below the middle shelf, providing location 5. Using the new structure in the experiment was associated with 10 percent fewer errors. The children who had not responded correctly on the first experiment to *under* and *underneath* but were correct on the second experiment used location 4, primarily, and held the red box on or over Cookie Monster's head. Some of the children who had missed *below* on the first experiment also used location 4 the second time, but they used locations 5 and 6 nearly as often as 4.

Having found that the altered structure with its new locations perhaps fit the children's mental images better, we were curious to see what the children would do who were correct the first time, who were able to use the necessary feature "lower in elevation than the reference object" to figure out that location 6 was the only possibility. Less than 5 percent chose location 6 for *under* and *underneath* in the second experiment. Ninety-four percent chose location 4 for *underneath* and 71 percent for *under,* but 80 percent chose location 5 for *below.* Clearly *under, underneath,* and *below* had qualities of meaning for these preschoolers in addition to the abstract feature, "lower in elevation than the reference object." It is impossible to be sure what the distinction is for them, but it looks as though they have encountered *under* and *underneath* in situations where the objects to be related were very close to each other vertically and "below" where the vertical distance is greater. The distinction that dictionaries draw between *under* or *underneath* and *below* (for one object to be *under* another, it must lie in the same vertical plane; this is not necessary for *below*), would probably not even be comprehensible to a preschooler. Figure 9.2 sketches the distinction.

SEMANTIC NETWORKS
FOR SPATIAL PREPOSITIONS

In the first experiment the only correct place to put Cookie Monster for *under, underneath,* and *below* was location 6. The children who responded correctly to two or three of these prepositions were responding to them as *synonyms,*

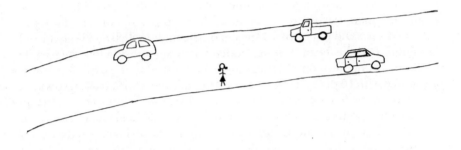

Erika is under/underneath the plane

The cars are all moving along below the plane

FIGURE 9.2. Under/underneath and below plane.

words that have the same meaning. Thirty-three percent of the children responded correctly on this experiment to all three prepositions, treating them as synonyms. In a related experiment (carried out in the same session) we asked the children to produce verbal concepts for *in, on, underneath, under,* and *below;* they were asked to tell a robot, who was just learning to talk, what each preposition meant. The children were successful most of the time. What was unexpected is that only three children produced verbal concepts like "*Underneath* means the same thing as *under,*" and "*Below* and *under* mean the same." Instead, for example, they responded with, "*Under* is underground," and "The foundation is *under* the house." These latter expressions link the prepositions to the child's experience and the real world. Verbal concepts like "*Under* means the same as *underneath,*" link the prepositions to each other to form a *semantic network.* Even though *under* means the same as *underneath* or *below* is implied by using the same location for the three prepositions in the comprehension task, only 6 percent gave evidence of having, in their minds, semantic networks linking *under, underneath,* and *below.* The other 94 percent of the children had verbal concepts that linked the words to the world and their experience rather than to other words (see Figure 9.3).

122

The level of cognitive processing does not produce (3) in response to 'tell' even though it is implied by (1).

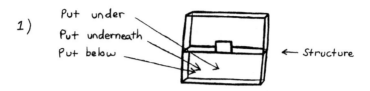

1)
Put under
Put underneath
Put below
← Structure

2)
Tell under ———→ "underground where miners go"
Tell underneath ———→ "underneath the bed"
Tell below ———→ "They're below, we're over."

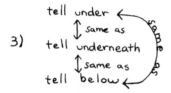

3)
tell under
↑ same as
tell underneath
↑ same as
tell below

FIGURE 9.3. Levels of cognitive processing for under, underneath, and below.

Recall that in Moran's study of word associations of Japanese and North American preschoolers and adults he found that American adults gave mainly logical associations. "Means the same" is, in Moran's terms, a logical relation, and our research on prepositions is consistent with Moran's in that our North American preschoolers did not give evidence of being able to directly relate verbal concepts, to have spatial prepositions semantically organized in terms of logical relations.

NATURAL CATEGORIES

I have briefly discussed verbal concepts of children as prototypical mental images that are formed automatically and effortlessly. I contrasted them with analytic featural concepts that are the result of purposeful, deliberate mental processing. I have mentioned that other animal species besides human beings are able to categorize stimuli (that is, select from a group of objects, pictures, and so on, subgroups) that belong together. The categorizing abilities of apes and pigeons are mentioned in Chapter Three.)

Let me digress for a moment to relate categories to verbal concepts. Pigeons in Herrnstein et al.'s experiment discriminated slides of trees (or parts of trees) from other slides. The pigeons had been conditioned to peck when slides showing trees or parts of trees were shown and not to peck to other slides. The ability of the pigeons to respond to the category "trees or parts of trees" was measured by their success in discriminating new slides showing trees or parts from other new slides; the abilities of apes to categorize have been demonstrated analogously. In Jeremy Anglin's work on verbal concept development in young children, he named the category "animal" and asked his subjects if the pictures he showed them (without naming them) were animals. The children said of the butterfly, "It's not an animal, it's a butterfly." Responding to the picture of the wombat, they said it was an animal. His research indicated that, for his subjects, the concept "animal" that underlies and names the category was perceptually determined.

I have described in Chapter Six how a syntactic operation, putting a word after an article to form a noun phrase, clues the child to a word's status as a common noun, the name for a class or category of "things." The question now is this: how is membership in the group named by the noun determined? Adults and older children have both mental images (perceptual concepts) and analytic featural verbal concepts for the same noun, concepts based on different rules for being an example of the concept. Some items that will be excluded from the child's mental image concept "animal," like butterflies and fish, will be included in the analytic featural concept.

Rosch and her colleagues (1973, 1976) have done a great deal of research to determine whether there are *natural* categories, based on characteristics of the real world that influence the way human beings classify phenomena. Rosch has written that the notion that human classification schemes are arbitrary systems imposed on the real world is incorrect. The occurrence of the features; Wings, feathers, beaks and two legs are highly correlated with each other (tend to occur together), and likewise fur and four feet. At the same time feathers and four feet, and wings and fur, are negatively correlated (tend not occur together). If an animal has feathers, it will not have four feet. The animals that have the highly correlated features form a natural category of animals. We call the category with wings "birds" and the category with fur "mammal." Having called the category with fur "mammal," we are immediately made aware of another characteristic of natural categories; they have fuzzy boundaries. Whales, which look like fish, belong to the analytic *featural* category, mammals. Natural categories and analytic featural categories overlap but are not identical. Most mammals will fall into both the perceptually (mental image) and featurally defined categories. Whales, porpoises, and other ocean dwelling mammals will fall into the featural but not the mental image category.

Rosch has proposed that natural categories have a core consisting of the best (prototypical) examples of the category surrounded by other members of the category of decreasing similarity to the prototypical examples. The more prototypical a member of the category is, the more features it has in common with other members of the category and the fewer with members of other categories. Thus, the whale is a mammal at the fuzzy boundary between mammals and fish. It has breathing, live birth, and nursing its young in common with the other mammals. It has its shape, absence of fur and feet, and its dwelling place in common with fish.

The concepts based on mental images of young children appear to consist of the central (prototypical) examples of categories.

The mental image and the analytic featural concept are two different kinds of concepts, or ways of organizing roughly the same contents of the mind in thinking and remembering. They are verbal concepts if the concept has a name so that, for example, hearing or seeing the word *dog* will retrieve from memory the mental image or verbal material about number of legs, warmblooded or not, type of coat, type of vocalization, and other features organizable as an analytic featural concept. The featural concept is a *proper set.* Membership in a class or proper set depends on having the particular groups of features that define the class or set. The whale is a borderline animal with the defining features of the mammal but with other features that are characteristic of fish, particularly the shape, lack of legs, and dwelling place. The natural concept of the whale is as a fish. In the ordinary experience of most human beings the whale is a fish. The concept of the whale as mammal is a learned concept. The system of classification of the earth's animals is the product of the science of biology. Each species and animal class is defined in terms of features, not all of which affect the animal's appearance, and the set of which has to be purposefully learned. When children are first learning the meaning of a word and developing a verbal concept from their ordinary experience, the concept will be a natural concept like the concept of the moon of the very young princess in James Thurber's fairy tale, *Many Moons.* The princess wanted the moon, and the wise men who know about the moon knew it could not be gotten for her. One of the court thought to ask the princess how big the moon was. She said that she knew it was quite small because when she held her thumb up between her eye and the moon, the moon was blocked from her view. This may seem an unusual and unlikely concept for the moon. But consider the concepts of the flat earth and the conceptualization of the universe with the earth in the center and the sun and the moon revolving around it. These were the prevailing concepts for centuries, and the heliocentric (sun-centered) concept of our solar system did not replace the earth-centered concept as the scientifically accepted concept until the sixteenth century.

Even now in my day-to-day life, although I "know" the earth is round, I use my natural concept that the world is flat as I go about my business. The sun rises and sets in my everyday thinking in accordance with my natural concept of the earth in relation to the sun and moon. When it was explained to me that the pictures of the moon taken by Luna 3 in 1959 showed the side of the moon that we on earth had never seen, I had to use my learned concept of the solar system to understand.

Before children go to school they have not, for the most part, developed learned featural concepts. Some of their naturally occurring concepts are shortlived or at least go underground because they are corrected by others. But we all say, including the meteorologist on the nightly news telecast, "sunrise will be at 6:10 tomorrow morning." So we know that there are natural concepts that people hang on to for everyday use, even though all the ones of us who have been through school also have learned concepts that organize the same contents of the mind but in the scientific way.

VERBAL CONCEPTS FOR CREATURES FROM OUTER SPACE

My students and I did an experiment several years ago to see how children and adults would categorize creatures from outer space. Our subjects were first graders, fifth graders, and college students. Our hypothesis was that first graders would use natural categories (like the classification of whales as fish) and fifth graders and college students would construct analytical categories based on features (like the classification of whales as mammals). We had three sets of creatures to classify called Snorbs, Gruffles, and Jexums. The pictures used for the Gruffles categorization task are shown in Figure 9.4.

Children who decided whether an unlabeled picture was a Gruffle on the basis of a natural category looked at an unlabeled picture, then at the pictures of Gruffles, and then at pictures of creatures from the other asteroids until they found a picture that "looked like" the unlabeled picture. The two pictures that were most often seen as looking alike were UGII and GIII. Roughly a fourth of our subjects matched these two and said "It's a Gruffle (UGI) because it looks like this one (pointing at GIII)."

Children who constructed analytical categories compared the Gruffles and the creatures from the other asteroids to find the defining features for Gruffles (tails, dots, and round eyes), the features that defined the proper set. We inferred this procedure from responses to UGII like, "Not a Gruffle, no tail," and to UGIII, "Gruffle, has an eye, freckles, and a tail."

In our subject sample 19 percent of first graders', 51 percent of fifth graders', and 88 percent of college students' responses were based on construction of analytical categories. (These differences were statistically significant, $P \leq .01$.)

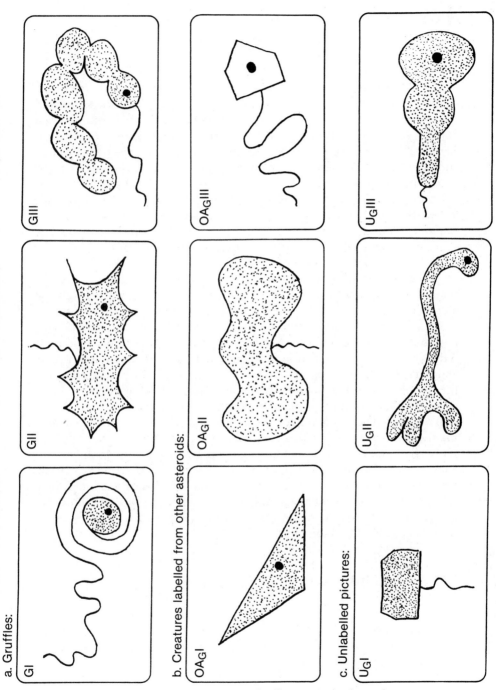

a. Gruffles:

GI

GII

GIII

b. Creatures labelled from other asteroids:

OA_GI

OA_GII

OA_GIII

c. Unlabelled pictures:

U_GI

U_GII

U_GIII

FIGURE 9.4. Stimuli for the Gruffles categorization task.

SEMANTIC DEVELOPMENT, COGNITIVE DEVELOPMENT, AND SCHOOLING

Perceptual matching on the basis of natural categories should be an expected strategy for first graders. It's use is in keeping with Anglin's findings, and it is the natural first response of most people when confronted with a novel object. "What does it look like?" is the first question to ask in finding out what an object is. This first question may be the only question asked by the young and unschooled. What causes people to ask further questions is their becoming dissatisfied with the results of their conceptualizing. That has occurred frequently in our history. Concepts get reorganized, by scientists for example, when it becomes clear that there are facts that the old concept cannot explain. The shift from the concept of the earth as flat to spherical came about because important predictions based on the flat earth concept were false. Boats did *not* sail off the edge of the ocean, never to return.

Sometimes ordinary experience leads us to reconceptualize. It looks as though the railroad tracks come together in the distance, but by walking along the tracks a long way, we can verify that the point at which the tracks look as though they meet keeps receding. In the lives of most people who have grown up in societies where children are educated in schools, schooling is the most important agent fostering conceptual change and development in children. In school, children learn to monitor their thinking, to ask themselves if their mental processing is achieving a good result. It has been suggested that self-monitoring of thinking (meta-cognitive awareness) is the skill or trait that differentiates the intellectual activity of schooled and unschooled persons and makes the cognitive functioning of educated people more effective than that of uneducated people. Semantic development, the subject of this chapter, is a component of cognitive development. Whenever the organization of the contents of the mind has a verbal aspect, it becomes not just a cognitive organization but more specifically a semantic organization, the development of which, through experience and/or maturation, is semantic development.

PARTIAL VERBAL CONCEPTS FOR TIMES PAST

This will be a very limited look at how children's language and communication regarding time is constrained by their cognitive development. There are many things people think about but are unable to put into words. All the mental processes of infants are nonverbal. Their thought processes are inseparable from their sensations and physical activity. As young children begin to learn words as names and to understand utterer's meaning of some of the sentences spoken to them; these verbal objects become part of their thought processes. But just because the child has the same word in his vocabulary as adults have or produces a phrase or sentence adults use does not mean that these verbal entities have the same meaning for the child as they have for an adult. Children's verbal concepts depend, in the first place, on their level of cognitive development. I overheard my four-year-old daughter tell her father,

1. Yesterday, I saw a duck cross the street.

and her friend, Stephanie,

2. Last night we had bacon.

She had seen the duck about half an hour before she recounted the experience, and she had eaten the bacon at breakfast on the day she was talking to Stephanie.

Even though my daughter had the same words in her vocabulary as adults have, the words did not reflect the same verbal understanding as the adults'. My daughter had had enough experience hearing *yesterday* and *last night* to induce part of their meanings but not enough experience to get the meaning precisely. Once she started a sentence to me with,

3. Last year before I was born . . .

I interrupted her to say,

4. Last year you were already born; you were three-years-old.

She replied indignantly,

5. I meant *very* last year.

She was gradually building up the meanings of the words, automatically associating the words to the experiences they accompanied and making assumptions about the range of experience the words referred to. This works for the child so that her automatically acquired verbal concepts match the adult ones in so many instances that we notice and remember mismatches. They are not likely to be common, physical object names because the child receives negative feedback, as my daughter did one night as we looked up at the full moon, and she said, "See egg." In order for a child to understand the extension (range) of a term, she has to experience positive and negative instances. Many times we are not aware that the child's verbal concept is being brought into conformity with the conventional concept. The child does not always use a word inappropriately to name an object or experience. The child thinks, but does not say, that the object in the sky is an egg. Later, the child hears someone else say, "Oh, look at the moon."

LEARNING WORD MEANINGS FROM SENTENCES

So far in talking about semantic development we have been concentrating mostly on (1) the relationship of word meaning to reality and (2) meanings of words organized in natural categories and proper sets. There comes a time in all our lives when we begin to learn increasingly the meanings of words primarily from the way they are used in sentences. We can do this because the meanings of the other words in the sentence are already known to us. We no longer, upon hearing a word or sentence, look around to see what is going on in order to figure out the meaning of what is being said. Instead we guess at the meaning of the new word from the context of the rest of the sentence or discourse. We begin to use language to learn language. A little child, hearing

1. He was a *mean* boy to pull the dog's tail,

might think *mean* meant *rash* or even *stupid.* After all the dog might bite.

2. It was a *mean* night out. That raw, cold wind froze my nose and ears.

Hearing (2) would make *rash* and *stupid* unlikely. Something that causes physical pain would be a possible definition for (1) and (2).

3. "I think you're *mean,*" Jody said to her mother when she told Jody she couldn't go to the party if she didn't clean up her room.

Sentence (3) alters the possible definition derived from (1) and (2), making it broader; *mean* causes pain, physical or mental. I am claiming that, in learning verbal concepts (word meanings), the learner unconsciously forms an hypothesis about word meaning from the sentence heard. The next sentence heard that contains the word provides positive or negative evidence about the hypothesis. If the evidence is negative, the learner changes the hypothesis.

Werner and Kaplan (1952) conducted an experimental investigation of the processes underlying the acquisition of word meanings from sentence contexts, like the example of *mean.* They, however, used invented nonsense words, and their sentences were constructed so that the six sentences for a nonsense word provided increasingly definite clues to the meaning of the word. They studied the acquisition of 12 nonsense words by five groups of 25 children each: 9, 10, 11, 12, and 13-year-olds. One of their nonsense words is shown in Table 9.2. Werner and Kaplan found that older children as compared to younger children were much better at figuring out the meanings of the nonsense words. The younger children were hampered by their difficulty in separating word meaning from sentence meaning. This may happen whenever the word learner does not hear the word in a variety of sentences. In my own case, I was surprised when I recently looked up *arcane*

TABLE 9.2. *Protema,* a Nonsense Word from Werner and Kaplan's Experiment on the Acquisition of Word Meaning

Protema (finish, complete)
1. To protema a job, you must have patience.
2. If a job is hard, Harry does not protema it.
3. Philip asked John to help him protema his homework.
4. John cannot protema the problem because he does not understand it.
5. You should try to protema your homework when it is only half done.
6. The painter could not protema the room because his brush broke.

Werner and Kaplan 1952.

in the dictionary to find that it means "secret." My definition based on the sentence(s) in which I had heard or read it had to do with savage rites of primitive people of long ago. *Arcane* must have been an adjective modifying rites in a sentence about primitive customs. The sentence context became part of my definition of *arcane,* and I did not read other sentences that would have caused me to eliminate from my definition the sentence context of primitive rites.

Most of the word meanings that we know have been acquired through our life experience, including reading, rather than through looking words up in the dictionary. Therefore it is always possible that some words will have different meanings for people because of different life experiences. Where it is really important to have a shared meaning for a word, parents of young children tend to check and make sure. Roger Brown has reported that the parents of Adam, Eve, and Sarah did not correct their children's grammar, but did correct them when they mispronounced words or said things that were not true. We can tolerate immature syntax as long as we can understand the child, but we want to be sure that meanings come through clear and true.

10
Reading

I came to the study of the reading process with the biases of the psycho-linguist. I thought that learning to read was the same as learning to speak, except that the code was different; the reading code is orthographic (based on spelling and the alphabet) instead of phonemic (based on the speech sounds of language). I became interested about the time that Jean Chall's work (1967) was becoming influential. Chall demonstrated that there were two aspects to learning to read that needed to be considered separately. The first thing the learner has to learn is to crack the orthographic code. Reading for meaning is the second aspect to reading, and success in it depends in part on having cracked the code. The child already knows from his life experience the relation between word sounds and word meanings. When the child learns in first grade to crack the orthographic code, he or she is learning the relation between the orthographic and phonemic codes (Table 10.1). If there are no words in the reading material presented to the beginning reader that are not in the child's spoken vocabulary, and the words are used in the kinds of sentences that have occurred in the child's language experience, then the task for the child is just code cracking. It sounded to me, a psycholinguist, straight forward and not too hard. The teacher teaches the child about phonics, and the child is started as a reader in the way he or she began as a speaker. Learning to read should be as easy as learning to speak, once the code is cracked, and for some children this is true. For others it is not. In coming to understand why some children have difficulty, we have arrived at a better understanding of learning to read. It is worth noting that the children who learn to read as readily as they had learned spoken language do not remember how they learned to read. It is the ones, like me, who had trouble who remember. I remember sitting at my desk one day toward the end of first grade with my book open to a story. We were having "silent" reading, and

TABLE 10.1. Phonemic Code, Meaning, and Orthographic Code

Phonemic code[a]	Meaning	Orthographic code
/dɔg/	four legged animal that barks and chases cats	dog
/rʌn/	to move on foot at a fast pace	run
/hat/	opposite of cold	hot

[a]I have written out the phonemic spellings, but what the child knows is just how the words sound.

our teacher was going from desk to desk looking over people's shoulders. She stopped at my desk and ran her finger under a sentence as she read the words. She made a comment, which I have forgotten. What I remember is a sinking feeling. Teacher's comment indicated that she thought I was actually getting meaning from the printing on the page. My problem was that I really did not understand how to read. I thought all I had to do was look at the printing on the page. I was a beginning reader in the days of the look-say method. The teacher had words printed on large cards (like flash cards for arithmetic). She would hold a card up for the class, say the word, and go on to the next card. Later in the year, she would ask a child the word when she held up the card. I had not been exposed to the alphabet. I do not remember being able to print my name.

My second memory is of sitting at home in the kitchen with my mother and my sister who was in kindergarten. I was looking at the word *grapes* in my reader and trying to sound it out. I said, "/gur//ē//pʌs/." My little sister said, "grapes." I have no further memories, so I assume that after that it was smooth sailing. My problem cleared when I learned that reading was an active process dependent on figuring out what the words on the page were, or as I would now say, cracking the orthographic-phonemic code. That is the beginning, but there are important differences between reading and talking besides the difference in code.

TOP-DOWN AND BOTTOM-UP PROCESSES IN READING

In my experience as a psycholinguist studying reading, becoming acquainted with the distinction between *top-down* and *bottom-up* processes greatly clarified issues. In the early 1970s, I read in the report of a conference on reading, "Good readers are good guessers," which implies that good readers are figuring out words on the basis of their sentence contexts rather than by stopping and sounding out words they do not recognize by sight (if they are beginning readers) to see if the words are in the their spoken vocabularies. About the same time a child I knew, a fourth grader, was beginning to experience grave problems in school. Her parents were told that their daughter had never really learned how to read. She had gotten along in the primary grades guessing at the meanings of words on the basis of sentence context and the pictures which accompany the text in early readers. Figuring out word meanings from sentence context is a *top-down* process; the reader is going from the higher level organization of sentence meaning to the lower level of word meaning. Getting at word meaning by sounding out the word is a *bottom-up* process. It is figuring out a word (a higher level of organization) from a sequence of phonemes (a lower level). If there are words and sentences from the beginning of learning to read, rather than simply isolated letters, both top-down and bottom-up processes need to be used. It is clear why the bottom-up processes are needed; these provide the elements of the code. What we read are letters, words, and sentences. We need the top-down processes because what we read for and understand, and what carries us along in reading, is meaning. It is not present in the letters and is barely glimpsed in the words, but it becomes more and more apparent as the sentences and paragraphs take shape.

The lowest level process specific to reading is letter perception. The model presented by Rumelhart and McClelland (1982) makes use of top-down and bottom-up processes to explain the perception of the letters in individual words. In their presentation Rumelhart and McClelland make use of three levels of information used by the reader in perceiving the letters of a word. These are the levels of the word, letter, and feature (Figure 10.1). The reader uses information from the feature and the word level in perceiving the letter. This comes about because the reader is acquiring information simultaneously at all three levels. It is partial information, but the letter perceived has to be consistent with this partial information, and this narrows the range of possibilities, perhaps to a single letter. In Figure 10.1, for example, the barely perceived features suggest a three letter word ending in *ut*. This ending is consistent with the word being *but, cut, gut, hut, nut,* or *put.* If the reader detects the feature, part of the letter extends below the line of type, the possibilities become limited to *gut* and *put.* Look at *but, cut, hut,* and *nut.* Their beginning letters do not have a part that extends below the line of type.

FIGURE 10.1. Top-down, bottom-up analysis to determine the letter in a word.

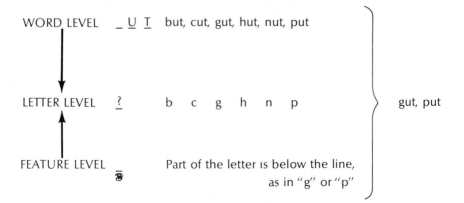

The interactional analysis has been applied to higher levels of processing involved in reading. (An excellent exposition is presented in M.J. Adams and A. Collins 1979.) In perceiving a word the reader makes use of information at the level of the letter and at the levels of syntax and semantics. I will carry on with the example of the perception of the letter to complete the three letter word ending in *ut*. If the word were being perceived as a word all by itself, or in a list, and therefore without context clues, the reader would have to continue examining the features of the letter for ones that differentiate *g* and *p*. The main one is that the part that extends below the line of type in *g* is an oval below the circle, whereas in *p*, it is a line on the left side of the circle. But if the word is part of a sentence, the context of the rest of the sentence clues the reader. If __ut is in the sentence, "That's my __ut reaction," the missing letter is *g*. If __ut is in the sentence, "Please __ut your knife on the table," the missing letter is *p*.

The reader acquires semantic context from the part of the text that he or she has already read and, in the case of primary grade readers, the pictures accompanying the text. From these, the reader will know, in a general way, what the text is about, or the *topic*. The reader will know, for example, whether it's about a trip to the moon, or Dick and Jane planting a vegetable garden. The reader will have vastly different expectations about what will appear on the printed page depending on whether the topic is a trip to the moon or planting a garden. All the top-down processes in reading are dependent on expectations derived from the context. Some are very low level expectations concerning the letters of a word or the words in a sentence. But topic determines high level expectations about the text and its content.

TOPIC FAMILIARITY

Readers' expectations as to the characteristics of text are strongly influenced by topic, and reading efficiency is enhanced if the reader is knowledgeable concerning the topic. If the reader is familiar with the topic, he or she is able to fill in gaps in the text that make reading difficult for the person who lacks the knowledge of the world that the text takes for granted. I have made up a little story using vocabulary and sentence structure appropriate for second graders. I am including it to demonstrate the importance of topic familiarity to reading comprehension.

Summer Vacation Fun

Erika and Raymond woke up very early. They could hardly wait to go clamming with their father. He had told them that low tide would be at eight o'clock this morning, so they would have to be down at the flats by seven. Raymond pulled on his trunks and ran out back of the cottage to look for his rake. Just then Father called,

"Hurry up, you two. I've got the pail and shovel." He came out the door and looked at Raymond and Erika.

"Erika, find your rake, and both of you put on your old sneakers."

The children hurried with their shoes, Erika found her rake, and they ran down to the beach. This was the first day of the Vivante family's summer vacation, and it was starting off just right.

The reader's ability to understand and remember the story depends, in part, on knowing about clamming. Knowledge related to hunting clams is summarized in Table 10.2.

If the reader is knowledgeable about family life in the United States, then family summer vacations, father-children activities, and appropriate clothing (swimsuits and tennis shoes) will be familiar. In short, if you are a child whose life experience has included family summer vacations and activities like those in the little story, you will be able to make sense of the story. Otherwise, the story may be hard to understand even if you can read the words. The second graders whose life experience has not included digging clams may not have *clamming, flats,* nor even *low tide* in their spoken vocabularies.

Research on reading (Anderson 1981) has shown that the reader's knowledge of the subject of the reading is the principal determinant of what will be understood and remembered. In his research, Anderson found that topic familiarity was more important than vocabulary difficulty. Knowing the meaning of technical words like *clamming* and *flats* is part of topic familiarity. Vocabulary difficulty refers to occurrence in the reading of less familiar

TABLE 10.2. Knowledge of Clamming Sufficient to Understand the Story

1. What are clams?
   Clams are shellfish that are good to eat.
2. Where found?
   Clams live in shallow ocean waters. Some live between the high and low tide lines, spending much of the time dug into the mud and sand.
3. When can they be hunted?
   They can be hunted during a period of time before and after dead low tide when the tide has gone out exposing the "flats," a muddy sandy area where clams may have dug themselves in.
4. How are clams hunted? (Clamming)
   Persons going clamming bring a pail, shovel, and rake to the flats at low tide. They look for a squirt of water coming out of the flats because squirts are made by clams. When they see a squirt, they dig up the sand and mud around it, pull the rake through the mud and sand, looking for clams. They put the ones they find in pails and continue looking for squirts and digging for clams until they have collected as many as they want.
5. Are there precautions to take?
   Because there are likely to be broken shells with sharp edges on the flats, it is wise to wear shoes.

words rather than more familiar ones with the same meaning, such as *amicable* instead of *friendly*. In other words Anderson found that how much children understood and remembered from what they had read depended more on whether the topic was familiar or unfamiliar (for top-down processing) than whether the vocabulary was familiar or unfamiliar (for bottom-up processing).

Along with topic familiarity, topic interest is important to children's reading comprehension. Children will be motivated to make an effort to read when the topic is of consuming interest to them.

READING INSTRUCTION

In addition to being mature enough to spend three or four hours sitting in a school room, being ready to learn to read means having had the experiences in life that give a child the vocabulary, grammatical knowledge, experience in making sense out of communications using language, and knowledge of the world that the school reading program assumes children have as they begin reading. Most American middle-class children come to school ready to learn to read texts that have been prepared with an eye to their experience. Children whose life experience has been different may not be ready, and teachers need to be aware of reading difficulties arising because a child's background knowledge does not have the ingredients that the reading material assumes. There are, however, differences between spoken and written language that will affect children even if difference in life experience is not a factor.

Written Language Instead of Spoken

For the most part spoken language is used in face-to-face conversation so that the people talking and listening have the time and place in common. They can observe each other's gestures and tone of voice. They share nonverbal information that clarifies verbal messages or indicates that clarification is needed (a quizzical look, for example), and that generally makes communication easier. In communication by written language, much more depends on characteristics of the text. The use in books of charts, diagrams, and pictures indicates that the written word is often not sufficient by itself. The beginning reader has to learn to get information from written language that comes with very little effort from spoken language. The extensive use of pictures in primary readers helps the new reader partly by providing information and partly by attracting the child's attention and getting him or her interested and motivated to do the sometimes difficult work of reading.

In addition to the difference in code (written rather than spoken) and the change from an interactive relationship (taking turns being both hearer and speaker) to being just reader, the beginner is faced with further challenges in learning to read. A crucial aspect to the problem of moving from spoken to written language is interpreting sentence structure from written materials. Sentence structure does not present problems in spoken language because it is clearly communicated by the stress and pitch patterns in utterances. We know whether a speaker is looking for an English soldier or a new garment by the stress on *red coat.* If the speaker says

1. I'm looking for a red coat,

it's the soldier.

2. I'm looking for a red coat,

means the garment.

The same patterns pertain for *White House,* the Presidents' residence, and *white house,* a house painted white. We usually do not mark stress and pitch patterns of written sentences. We get some clues from punctuation.

3. You're going to school

is a question or a statement depending on whether it is punctuated with a question mark or a period. But the question of whether the red coat is a person or a garment is answered by contextual information including the topic of the text in which the sentence appears.

Another syntactic problem for the beginning reader is the greater complexity of written sentences compared to spoken ones. Sentences like

4. I saw the little green man who wanted an egg for supper

do not present a problem for the skilled reader. A beginner, however, is likely to read:

4a. I saw the little green man.

and

4b. Who wanted an egg for supper?

as two separate sentences, (4a) and (4b). Sentence (4b) is a question that is a confusing nonsequitor if (4a) is read as a complete sentence. In a sentence such as

5. I want a cookie to eat with my ice cream.

a beginning reader is likely to expect the sentence to end with

5a. I want a cookie.

The reader may attempt to start a new sentence with

5b. to eat my ice cream

and again be confused. If children have been read books that have complicated sentences (but ones they are really interested in), they will be prepared to meet complicated sentences in their own reading.[1]

Word Recognition

Currently much research on early reading is concerned with word recognition, what the child has to learn to do, rather than code cracking, a method that will lead to the result—word recognition. If we think in terms of word recognition, we are alerted to both top-down and bottom-up processes. We do not neglect the child's learning letter-to-sound correspondences. Learning these is crucial to the child's being able to figure out the meaning-spelling relationship of words he or she is encountering for the first time in reading words that are in his or her spoken vocabulary. If the child can crack the spelling-sound code, the meaning-spelling relationship is revealed. This is the goal of early reading, but we do not have research results that indicate how best to teach early reading. Should we directly teach letter-to-sound correspondences (phonics), or should we teach whole words (look-say)? We know we want children to learn the letter-to-sound correspondences, phonics, but they are extremely tedious to learn. On the other hand if we teach the look-say method, we have the enormous advantage that words have meaning and that meaning makes learning interesting. But some children may not learn letter-sound relationships from look-say teaching so that they can figure out new words. Experience leads us to think we need some of both phonics and look-say teaching. Directly teaching phonics (but not a burdensome amount) indicates to the child what the bottom-up procedure is (if, like me, the child does not understand).

Spelling

When I was a child, spelling as a school subject consisted of weekly spelling tests of words that a person needed to be taught to learn to spell. The list of words was gone over in class to make sure everyone knew the meanings of the words and the tricky things about their spelling. I remember that the *e* in *judge* is dropped before adding *ment* to form *judgment,* while other words like *move* keep the *e* as in *movement.* Spellings were separately learned by rote.

Another development of the 1970s is the use of the subject of spelling to

---

[1] I found *Born Free* by Joy Adamson excellent to read to seven- and eight-year-olds. It is interesting to children, and its sentences are complicated.

teach common spelling patterns and word-part sounds in English; for example, *tion* as in *creation* and *nation* is pronounced /šʌn/. This is a further aid to the child in meeting unfamiliar words in reading; now the child may be able to determine the pronunciation of a new word because it is built on well-known spelling patterns. The meanings of new words have to be worked out on the basis of topic and sentence context, dictionary, and teacher help. Spelling is to reading as speaking is to listening in that it is an *encoding* rather than *decoding* process. Seeing the close link of spelling to reading and becoming aware that common spelling patterns of English can be taught beginning readers has brought about what appears to be a new method for helping the beginning reader induce rules, in this case rules of English spelling. We saw in the discussions of the child's acquisition of English grammar (the rules for forming the plural, the past tense, and so on, the syntactic operations of verbs, count nouns, and mass nouns) that children regularly induce these rules just by having language used meaningfully with them. Some children also acquire the letter-sound correspondence rules and the common spelling pattern rules pretty much on their own. A teacher in a private school in Washington, D.C. has told me that about 10 percent of the children coming to her school are self-taught readers. They are read to by parents and others. They rapidly learn the text of their favorite picture books by heart (as many children do), and this provides them with the material— written text, its sounds, and meanings—to figure out the phonemic-orthographic correspondences and to become readers.

The majority of children are not self-taught readers and require more or less help. The principal of my neighborhood's elementary school in Lexington, Massachusetts, has told me that the school's reading program starts in kindergarten where children are taught to recognize consonants as letters of the alphabet and consonant-sound relations. Games are played in which children take turns saying the names of things beginning with a particular consonant. Children who are ready are then taught vowel names and vowel-sound relations. In first grade both whole word sight-sound relations (the look-say method) and letter-sound relations are taught. Children having difficulty are taught using readers designed to include many words having the same spelling pattern: *may, day, fan, man, can,* and so on. Spelling as a school subject (learning the common spelling patterns in English) is regarded as useful to all children. Fourth to eighth graders (skilled readers), use word growth spelling kits, self-correcting "spellers" that teach less common spelling patterns in English. The statements of these two persons involved with teaching reading suggest that there are various degrees of ability in learning to read and that tailoring instructional techniques to children's varying capacities pays off. Reading is a skill, and some children require a great deal of practice acquiring the skill. I have tutored one child who, it was apparent at Christmas of her year in first grade, was not learning to read in school. A carefully graduated series of interesting readings was worked out for her. She read aloud to me for ten minutes every day before school started. I helped by saying things like, "Little Miss A says her name," if the child didn't realize that the *a* in *tale* is long. Or I said, "Little Miss A says / æ /. . . ." if the problem was the *a* in *tattle*. Sometimes I provided an entire word like *robot*. I never stated rules. I just provided the occasion for steady, nononerous practice, and the skill developed over the next year and a half so that by third grade the child was a "good" reader. I should mention that she was read to from such books as *Born Free* so that she became used to the complex syntax of written English.

Reading Groups

In the primary grades the majority of school children are placed in reading groups. The children in a group take turns reading aloud from a story in their reader. A reading specialist in the Lexington, Massachusetts, school system said to me, "Children don't learn to read in reading groups; the teacher finds out who *can't* read." If you had the experience of being in a reading group, you probably remember. Except when you were the one reading out loud, you were not paying close attention unless you had exactly the same problems with the text as the child doing the reading. Otherwise you didn't get anything out of listening to a child read and to the teacher's correcting him or her.

Early Readers

The quality of readers widely used in reading programs in this country is poor (R. Anderson, as cited by R. Weinsten 1982). In trying to make them easy to read, editors have made them confusing and uninteresting. To avoid complex sentences and conjunctions, editors turn complex sentences into simple sentences.

   6. Little duck got up at three o'clock in order to get the worms before the snake woke up.
   6a. Little duck got up at three o'clock.
   6b. He got the worms.
   6c. The snake woke up.

This is an example constructed to show that transforming (6) into (6a), (6b), and (6c) eliminates little duck's motivation and planning, which are conveyed by *in order to* and *before*. The series of simple sentences makes the event look like a lucky accident. A better way to help children deal with the problems posed by complex sentences and conjunctions is to read to beginning readers interesting stories that contain the complex sentences and conjunctions so they have experience with complicated syntax before they meet it in their reading.

Restricting the vocabulary of early readers to a small number of high frequency words means that there won't be exciting ingredients like robots and space ships in the stories. I can remember that my son, when he was in first grade, was asked by a friend of mine what the children in his reader did. "Mostly look and run," he replied.

Reading Disability

Suppose that reading comes as naturally as talking for some children; for others, it is only necessary to give them a minimal introduction to letter-sound decoding or to teach a 25 word sight vocabulary to have them reading. Suppose that there is a third group that needs a couple of months of phonics and/or whole word instruction to master the first reader. All of these children will work on their reading skill and must understand what they are doing by Christmas vacation in first grade. Any child in the class who is not working on the skill and does not understand what reading is by this time will have the experience of *not* learning the skill that school, especially first grade, is mostly about; the child will also have the experience of *not* understanding what the children who can read are actually doing. This is a devastating experience and is very destructive to the child's self-esteem; it is likely to make the child unwilling to continue to try.

Even though we have seen progress in the understanding of the process of reading, we still do not have a good understanding of the reasons why so many children have trouble learning to read. Over the years, theories have been proposed attributing specific reading disability, a disability not due to emotional problems, mental retardation, or any general cause, to brain dysfunctions of one kind or another. However, as late as 1980 (Valtin 1980) there was no concensus concerning the cause(s) of specific reading disability, and I do not feel it is worthwhile to discuss the current theories. Rather, I will conclude by stating my conviction that more individualized instruction and interesting reading practice for children to whom reading does not come easily is a strategy that deserves a good try.

11

Bilingualism and Second Language Learning

Bilingualism and second language learning are complex topics, and it is probably useful to introduce them with a bit about the reasons for bilingualism and for learning a second (or more) languages. In many parts of the world at various times an informal language and a formal language have existed together. When a number of separate communities speaking different languages have political, religious, or other reasons for communicating with each other, they need a language for these purposes. In Europe until the middle of the seventeenth century, Latin was the formal language. English, French, and German, for example, were spoken in local regions, but Latin was the language of the church, government, courts, and for conducting relations between political units. During the Middle Ages, the church, whose language was Latin, was the institution that prevented the total collapse of civilization. Most people could not read or write and spoke only the language of their speech communities. Only a very few people, mainly the clergy, some scholars, and a few of the nobility, learned to read and write as well as speak Latin.

By the middle of the seventeenth century France had become the dominant political and economic power in Europe and the French language replaced Latin as the *lingua franca* (language used as a medium of communication between people of different languages) for official, formal purposes in Europe.

When a group of separate states, principalities, or tribal groups speaking different languages form a nation, they have to adopt a common language. In Tanzania, Swahili has become the national language. In China, the government of Mao made Mandarin the national language and the language of instruction in the schools. Pilipino, a version of Tagalog, has been established in the Republic of the Philippines as the national language.

145

Russian is the *lingua franca* of the USSR, a nation in which 130 different languages are spoken in its 15 republics. Many people in the USSR do not speak Russian, and especially since 1970, the central government has sought to have Russian taught in school as the second language in the non-Russian speaking parts of the Soviet Union. In the United States we have not had a national language policy. Early in our history there were Spanish, French, and Dutch speaking communities. These languages were superceded by English as political domination of the country fell to Britain.

When a nation is formed and a national language is established without the willing compliance of local language/culture communities, the resistance of the communities to the political development is frequently expressed by an intense interest in the local language and customs. The identity of the people as members of a particular group is maintained by speaking and teaching their children the "old" language and keeping up the old customs.

Today, bilingualism is common in many parts of the world where countries (or speech communities) are small and where, in day-to-day life, members of one speech community are in contact with members of another community. Italian, German, and French are the languages of the different cantons (states), of Switzerland. People who do business throughout the country acquire a certain fluency in the two languages that are not the principal language of their canton. I say a *certain* fluency because I do not want to make a claim that the Swiss become equally fluent in all languages. That depends on the extent of their use of the nonmother tongues (languages not their first language). Do they use the nonnative languages only for business purposes? Do they read and write the nonnative languages? The answers to these questions tell a great deal about how bilingual a person is.

In addition to bilingualism based on speech communities in day-to-day contact, there is also the bilingualism based on learning. Second languages are acquired in the course of education and scholarly work. People become bilingual in order to work in the foreign service of their countries. They learn second languages in order to study the work of foreign scholars, poets, and scientists.

LEARNING A SECOND LANGUAGE

In the United States second language familiarity based on learning is more widespread than bilingualism based on day-to-day contact. Typically students in American secondary schools, and to a lesser extent in primary schools, are taught foreign languages. Foreign language teaching has been more successful for purposes of reading and writing than for day-to-day living. When a foreign language is learned for reading and writing the emphasis is on translation from the foreign language to English (reading) and from English to the foreign language (writing). When a foreign language is learned for living, under optimal circumstances, translation between English and the foreign language is avoided. The learning is made to approximate first language learning in that only the target language (the language to be learned) is ever used—along with pointing, pantomine, pictures, and real world objects, relations, and experience that language glosses.

In the public primary school system in Paris, France, there is one school in each district (arrondisement) that has a class to initiate all foreign primary school students in the French language. Children are from many different countries, and their only means of communicating with each other is their emerging French. This provides a powerful social motivation for learning and at the same time makes it unintimidating since everyone in the class is just learning French. As soon as they are fluent, the children are moved into the regular class. In 1979, a third grader and fifth grader (both boys) attended such a class in the 16th arrondisement in Paris. The fifth grader was placed in grade "huitieme" in January. The third grader remained in the adaptation class the entire year. His parents were told that he also could have been placed in the regular class in January but the class was too crowded. The boys' father told me that, by the end of the school year, both boys were culturally integrated, knew the French slang, and socialized with the French children. The younger boy's English, however, was beginning to slip a little through lack of use.

In my thinking, a person has truly acquired a second language when he or she can think in the language—which means, when the person does not need to mentally translate into English to understand or to consciously construct an utterance in the second language in order to say something. This happens to people who live in a foreign country, associate mainly with speakers of the target language, read and write the target language, and avoid having anything to do with English speakers, books, and so on. Two college-age women described this experience to me, one with French and the other with Italian. After six months of total immersion in the language, schooling, and life of the foreign country—a difficult, tiring, and wearing time when they had to concentrate on forming their utterances and on listening to others—each awoke one day and found she didn't have to work at it anymore. She didn't have to think out what she was going to say. It came naturally, just like English. This must be the experience of all those who become fluent in a second language, including all of the adult immigrants to the United States who learn to speak, read, and write English, even though they always speak English with an accent. The processing becomes automatic, and the speaker can concentrate on what he or she wants to say and not on how to say it.

UGUISU LEARNS ENGLISH

Uguisu, which means "nightingale" in Japanese, is the name Kenji Hakuta (1974, 1975) gave to a five-year-old Japanese girl. Hakuta studied Uguisu's acquisition of English as a second language. Uguisu and her parents lived for two years in a working class section of Cambridge, Massachusetts. Play with the children of the neighborhood was Uguisu's primary source of experience in hearing and speaking English. She attended public kindergarten two hours a day and later elementary school where she was given no explicit instruction in English. Hakuta tape recorded (and subsequently transcribed) two hour, biweekly samples of Uguisu's speech as she interacted with neighborhood friends. The transcripts provided Hakuta with a sample, over time, of Uguisu's speech in English so he could analyze how it developed.

One of the characteristics of Uguisu's developing English that Hakuta studied was her use of word sequences that occur frequently in people's speech. Hakuta was interested in the sequences that looked grammatically well-formed. Looking at

1. All these are sick.
2. Why these are dirty?

you would think that Uguisu understood that the subject and the verb in an English sentence must have number agreement (they both must be plural or both singular). Hakuta makes the claim and supports it with data that, when Uguisu began using *these are* and *this is,* they were memorized as chunks rather than spontaneously produced by Uguisu to form a sentence. His evidence is that, in the early weeks, Uguisu did not respect the rule of number agreement in using them. She said *these is* as well as *these are.* She used *this is* in talking about several objects as in "this is my dolls," and she used *these are* in referring to one object. Hakuta has tabulated for the first 15 of Uguisu's biweekly speech samples the number of times Uguisu used (1) *this is* when she should have used *these are,* (2) *these are* correctly and (3) *these are* incorrectly. Comparing Uguisu's first 11 speech samples with her next four, he found that she was as likely to be wrong as correct (as far as number agreement is concerned) in the first 11 samples, with 66 incorrect and 61 correct uses of *this is* and *these are.* In the next four samples there were seven correct instances and no incorrect instances.

In the early period, even though Uguisu used *these are* and *this is,* she used them correctly less than half of the time. She used *these are* and *this is* because she heard these patterns used by her friends. She had learned the sentence context in which the general pattern belonged, but she had not induced the rule, subject and verb agree in number. Beginning with sample 12, there are no mistakes with *this is* and *these are* in her speech samples.

Hakuta presents evidence that *do you* was also a *prefabricated pattern,* a memorized chunk when Uguisu began to use it. She said,

3. How do you do it?
4. Do you want this one?

but also,

5. What do you do it, this, froggie?
6. What do you drinking, her?

Hakuta concluded that (5) and (6) represent Uguisu's attempts to form questions with third person subjects: froggie and her. "What is froggie doing," and "What is she (her) drinking," might be syntactically correct versions of Uguisu's questions.

Hakuta proposed that Uguisu (and other second language learners) use prefabricated patterns, which they have rote-learned as though they were single words, in the early stages of second language acquisition. As the learner grasps syntactic patterns in the target language, the prefabricated patterns as memorized chunks are no longer used where they are incorrect. I think Hakuta is correct. When a language is learned orally with no explicit teaching of syntax, as Uguisu learned English, the learner's decision about what is a word and what is the variable part of a verb that changes depending on whether it's second or third person (or present or some other tense) may have to be revised as familiarity with the language grows. It is true not only of second language learners like Uguisu but also of children learning their native language. The second language learner's acquisition of the syntax of the target language is complicated by the syntactic system of the learner's native language. This is a subject we will return to, but first, I want to describe Shirley Loveland's study of native French speakers' learning English in a Canadian kindergarten.

FRENCH-SPEAKING KINDERGARTNERS LEARNING ENGLISH

Loveland (1974) studied the acquisition of the English negative by French speakers in a total immersion English kindergarten. Her question was whether a French speaking child of kindergarten age has to go through the same developmental stages of language in acquiring English as native English speakers go through in the first four years of life. Or is it possible for the French speaker to make a transfer from his or her established French syntax to a relatively advanced stage of English syntax? Loveland studied negation for which stages of development have been formulated for English (Klima and Bellugi 1966) and French (Vaillancourt 1968). Loveland poses the issue in this way: a child who does not speak the language of the children who are his or her playmates will rapidly develop some competence in the playgroup's language. How does a child do it? Assume the child (as in Loveland's study) has mastered French syntax; if the playmates have mastered English syntax so that the competent French speaking child hears syntactically correct English, does the French child begin to speak syntactically correct English, or does the child go through the stages of learning a second language that native speakers go through?

The stages in the development of negation in English are

Stage 1

The negative comes either at the beginning or end of the utterance.

> no fall
> more no
> not a teddy bear

Stage 2

At Stage 2 the negative can be within the utterance although some utterances are still governed by the stage one rule. In addition to *no* and *not, can't* and *don't* are negative elements.

> I can't see you.
> Don't leave me.
> I don't like . . .
> I no want . . .

Stage 3

By Stage 3 the child has mastered the English auxiliary system for verbs so that he or she uses the negatives *won't, can't,* and *didn't,* as well as *will, do, can,* and so on. Negative pronouns *(none, no one, nothing)* are rare. The change from *some* to *any* with negation is not mastered. Children say, "I don't want some" rather than "I don't want any." Rules of Stage 1 and 2 continue to be used.

> I didn't did it.
> I don't want some supper.
> Donna won't let go.
> I'm not crying.

There are two main negative forms in French: *non* and *ne. Non* is used by itself to indicate a negative response.

Pouvez vous m'aider?	Non.
Can you help me?	No.
a gauche?	Non, a droit.
Left?	No, right.

Non is found in negative expressions.

non seulement
not only
non plus
not anymore

When the negative element is within the utterance, its form is *ne* immediately preceding the verb and *pas* following the verb if the verb or the statement as a whole is being negated.

Je *ne* le veux *pas.*
I don't want it.
Anne ne voit pas l'arbre.
Anne doesn't see the tree.

Less commonly, *ne point* is used for emphasis to indicate *not one bit* or *not at all.*

Je ne le veux *point.*
I don't want it at all, a bit.

Other common negative forms include *ne jemais, never; ne que, only; ne rien, nothing;* and *ne personne, no one.*

Il *ne* reste *jamais* chez lui.
He never stays home.

In informal spoken French the element *ne* is sometimes uttered so rapidly it can scarcely be heard, and at other times it is omitted entirely.

"Je sais *pas*" is said instead of "je *ne* sais *pas.*"
I don't know

On the basis of her study of negatives used by native French speakers between three and five years of age, Vaillancourt formulated a three-stage account of acquisition of negation in French.

Stage 1

Stage 1 is marked by strong use of the negative, *non.* Even when *pas* is part of an utterance, *non* precedes it. *Non* and *pas* are the negative elements. *Ne* is omitted.

Non, je suis pas un bebe.
No, I am not a baby.
Non, non, c'etait du lait.
No, no, it's milk.

(This should be, " 'C'etait *pas* du lait.")
(It's not milk.)

Stage 2

Utterances are longer and the strong use of *non* disappears. Negations now appear in somewhat awkward interrogative sentences.

> Tu l'sais pas c'est quoi le nom du cochon.
> You don't know it; what the pig's name is?
> Tu sais pas c'est marque quoi, hein?
> You don't know what's written, right?
> C'est pas bien, hein, Maman?
> It's not good, right, Momma?

Stage 3

By Stage 3 children use a wider range of negative elements including *rien, jamais,* and *non plus.* They are able to construct sentences with two negations. They have not learned that if *rien, jamais,* and so on, are the negatives, *pas* should not appear also. The negative element *ne* is not used. It is not surprising that *ne* is not used since it is so frequently absent in adult informal speech.

> J'irai pas jamais a l'ecole.
> I will never go to school
> C'est pas des vrais sous, je peux pas rien acheter.
> It's not real pennies; I can't buy anything.

The subjects of Loveland's research were native French speakers attending English language kindergartens in Quebec province, Canada. They ranged in age from five years, eight months to six years, six months with an average age of six years, one month. The study was carried out in June, the end of the school year. Eleven of the families spoke only French at home; the other three made some use of English. Five of the children spoke no English when they entered kindergarten. The English of the other nine ranged from a few words of English to relative fluency.

The two kindergarten teachers were fluent bilinguals whose first language was English. The three kindergarten classes (one teacher taught two) emphasized self-directed rather than teacher-directed activities, and there was a great deal of social interaction and conversation among the children. Control of English negation was assessed on the basis of the children's responses in a game about a little boy who always said no. On another day the same game was played with each child in French so that Loveland had data to compare each child's mastery of negation in both French and English.

Before the game was played individually with the children, it was played (using negative forms not used for the individual assessments) in class with all the children together. The individual sessions began with Loveland saying to the child, "Do you remember the game we played in class about the little boy who always says no? Now I'd like to tell you some more things, and you tell me what he said. His mother said, "Please eat your carrots." He said, "No, I won't eat my carrots." Loveland encouraged the child to join in the response. After this little warmup, Loveland said eight sentences and tape recorded the child's response to each. The entire list of sentences in English and French is given in the appendix to this chapter. The first sentence was

1. When his friend said, "That's a jet," he said _____.
   (Expected response: "No, that's not a jet.")

Again on another day the game was played individually with the children, using the same warmup, but this time in French. "Te rappeles-tu du jeu du petit garçon qui disait toujours non? . . ." The eight sentences were then said and responded to in French by each of the 14 children.

Each child's English responses were classified according to Klima and Bellugi's stages and those in French according to Vaillancourt's stages. Loveland calculated French and English proficiency scores for the 14 children based on their percentage of required Stage 3 responses in each language. (Details of the calculations are given in the appendix to the chapter.) The children's proficiency scores and information about their language experience are presented in Table 11.1. Only six of the children had high or good scores in French proficiency and only six in English; only Benoit and Sylvain were proficient in both. The home language of both children was French only. Both had attended an English nursery school.

Loveland's findings raise several questions for our consideration. First, there is Loveland's own question: can a person proficient in his or her native language directly acquire corresponding proficiency in a second language without going through the stages that a very young child who is learning the language as his or her native language goes through. Loveland's findings suggest that the question needs to be more precisely formulated. First, the length of time or the amount of exposure to the second language necessary for acquiring its syntax needs to be specified. Perhaps attending an English language kindergarten for a school year does not provide the necessary experience with English for proficiency to develop. Table 11.1 shows that no child who came to kindergarten without previous experience with English, either at home or in nursery school, became proficient in English. Kindergarten does not take up much of a child's day. If most of the rest of the day is spent speaking French, it interferes with mastering English. It's not that these children did not respond in English but rather that their responses were not grammatical.

Table 11.2 gives the responses of Claude, high in English proficiency and low in French, and Anne, low in English and high in French. Claude is

TABLE 11.1. English and French Proficiency of Native French Speakers in an English Kindergarten

Name	English Proficiency[a]	French Proficiency	Home language	Preschool experience with English	Teacher rating of English on entering school
Benoit	High	Good	French only	English nursery school	Quite fluent
Claude	High	Low	French only	English district residence and playmates	Quite fluent
Linda	High	Low	French generally, some English	English nursery school, mother bilingual	Quite fluent
Patrick	High	Low	French generally, some English	Mother bilingual	A little English
Alan	Good	Low	French generally, some English	Father bilingual	A little English
Sylvain	Good	High	French only	Two months in English nursery school	A little English
Stephane	Low	Low	French only	Bilingual nursery school	A few words
Eric	Low	Good	French only	Bilingual nursery school	A few words
Peter	Low	Low	French only	Older brother bilingual	A few words
Philippe	Low	Good	French only	None	No English
Luce	Low	Low	French only	None	No English
Daniel	Low	High	French only	None	No English
Patrice	Low	Low	French only	None	No English
Anne	Low	High	French only	None	No English

[a]High, 80–100% Stage 3; good, 60–79%; medium, 40–59%; low, below 40%.
Loveland 1974

TABLE 11.2. Claude and Anne's English and French Negative Responses

Claude	
1. Not a jet.	Non, ce n'est pas un jet.
2. No, I'm not going to sleep.	Non, je ne dors pas.
3. No, I haven't been to Montreal.	Non.
4. No, I'm not a good boy.	Non, je n'est pas un bon garçon.
5. No, I don't want to paint.	Non, je ne veux pas peinturer.
6. No, you can't.	Non, tu ne peux pas grimper dans cet arbre.
7. No, there's nobody home.	Non, il n'y a pas quelqu'un ici.
8. No, there's nothing.	Non, il y a rien dans ta poche.
Anne	
1. No, not a jet.	Non, pas un jet.
2. No, I no asleep.	Non, je ne dors pas.
3. No, Montreal.	Non, j'ai jamais été à Montreal.
4. Not good boy.	Non, je ne suis pas un bon garçon.
5. No, I no paint.	Non, je ne veux pas peinturer.
6. Not a tree.	Non, tu ne peux pas grimper dans cet arbre.
7. No.	Non, y a personne ici.
8. No.	Non, il n'y a rien dans ta poche.

Loveland 1974

low in French proficiency because he failed to give a Stage 3 response to (3) and (7). He did respond with a Stage 3 response to (8), the other French question requiring a Stage 3 response. He responded at Stage 3 to five of the six English questions requiring Stage 3 responses. He missed on (1). Anne failed to give Stage 3 responses to any of the six English questions requiring them (1, 2, 3, 4, 7, and 8); (5) and (6) require only Stage 2 responses because *don't* and *can't* are acquired at Stage 2 as negatives. She gave Stage 3 responses to all the French questions requiring them (3, 7, and 8).

PSYCHOLOGICAL AND SOCIAL BARRIERS TO LEARNING A SECOND LANGUAGE

Whether it is hard or easy to learn a second language partly depends on how the learner feels about the people who speak the language and their culture in relation to him or herself. If the person (1) likes and admires the people who speak the target language, (2) wants to be friends with them and (3) feels that they will like him or her and his or her people and be friendly, learning the target language will be easier than if the language learner has reservations about (1), (2), or (3). Since Loveland's subjects were placed in English kindergartens by their parents, voluntarily, we can assume that the parents

TABLE 11A.1. Comparison of Stage 3 Responses in Both Languages

English (6 possible)				French (3 possible)
100%		High		
Benoit	6		Anne	3
			Daniel	3
			Sylvain	3
83%		High		
Claude	5			
Linda	5			
Patrick	5			
66%		Good		
Alan	4		Philipp	2
Sylvain	4		Eric	2
			Benoit	2
33%		Low		
Stephane	2		Luce	1
Eric	2		Peter	1
Peter	2		Stephane	1
Philippe	2		Alan	1
Luce	2		Linda	1
Daniel	2		Claude	1
16%		Low		
Patrice	1			
Anne	0	Low	Patrick	0
			Patrice	0

Loveland 1974

want the children to learn English. It probably means that (1), (2), and (3) are true of the parents. When people learn a new language because they are refugees from their native lands either because of war, persecution, or political unrest, they may have mixed feelings about the country in which they settle. The customs, values, and way of life may be very different from those of their native countries. They may be homesick and unsympathetic to the ways of the people of the new country. The longing for one's native land, the feeling that one's human identity is as an Argentinian, Hungarian, and so on, creates a psychological barrier to becoming a proficient speaker of a new language. A friend who became a citizen of the United States after leaving Poland to escape the Nazis once said to me, "If I lost my accent I wouldn't be Polish anymore. I would lose my identity." She has lived in the United States for 40 years and yet her sense of self is tied to being Polish. However, people who choose to emigrate and become citizens of a new country may be eager for an identity as citizens of their chosen country. They may not have nostalgic feelings creating a psychological barrier to learning the new (target) language. (This will be true for many refugees, also.)

Social barriers arise from factors that prevent good relations between the group who speak the target language and the group learning it. For example, there are strong, negative social attitudes separating English-speaking Americans from Spanish-speaking migrant workers in the southwestern United States. According to John Schumann (1978), a bad situation for acquiring a second language exists when the immigrant group and the population in the new country (1) have conflicting cultures, (2) have negative attitudes toward each other, (3) and do not want to see the immigrant group assimilated in the new country. Acquiring a second language is hampered further when (4) the immigrant group is large and cohesive, and (5) it does not plan to remain in the new country over a long period of time. Any one of these factors will raise a social barrier to the learning of the new language by the immigrant group. If the groups have nonconflicting cultures, positive attitudes toward each other and want to see the immigrant group assimilated in the new country, and if the immigrant group is small, not cohesive, and plans to remain in the new country, social barriers to the immigrants' learning the new language are greatly reduced.

SECOND LANGUAGE LEARNING RESEARCH

There is considerable interest in the United States at this time in second language learning. The interest derives in part from the influx of refugees— speakers of Vietnamese, Khmer, Thai, Hmong, and Chinese from the Far East; speakers of Russian from the U.S.S.R.; and speakers of Spanish from Cuba. More important than these, perhaps, are the Spanish speakers from Puerto Rico and Mexico, many of whom have lived in the United States a long time without being successfully integrated into the culture. Perhaps the most apparent problem for Hispanics as a group has been difficulty with English. After discussing second language learning I want to conclude this chapter with a short consideration of bilingual education, which has frequently been proposed as the best way to enable the native Spanish speakers in the Southwest, particularly, to overcome their difficulties in becoming ac-culturated in the United States. In order to most effectively teach English to the refugees and immigrants to the United States, we need to understand what the process is in learning a second language. In the early 1970s, the theory was that the learner acquired language as a set of habits. To the extent that the grammar of the second language is like the learner's native language, there is *positive transfer* of habits from first to second language, and all that has to be learned anew is vocabulary. If the grammars of the two languages are different, there is *negative transfer,* and the learner will make errors in speaking the target language based on *interference.* The learner will construct utterances based on grammatical habits from his or her first language. This method of analyzing second language learning is called *contrastive analysis.* The implication for second language teaching is that vocabulary and grammatical patterns in the new language should be practiced by the learner so that new habits will be formed; drill is particularly useful. Research on the types of speaking errors by persons learning a second language indicated that a large proportion were not caused by interference but were the kind of errors that young children make in the process of learning their first language. Contrastive analysis has given way to *error analysis,* defined as analysis of all systematic deviations of the learner's language from the way it is spoken by native speakers (Hakuta and Cancino 1980). The second language learner is seen as proceeding through a series of intermediate grammars as he or she acquires the second language. Some of the systematic errors are interference errors. The other two types, which also are made by children learning a first language, are *overgeneralization* and *simplification* errors. Overgeneralization errors occur when the plural of *foot* is given as *foots* or the past tense of *go* as *goed.* Among Philippe's English responses (Table 11.2),

7. No, I not asleep
8. No, I not a good boy

are simplification errors. Philippe has not supplied *am,* required in both sentences. This is the kind of error that is typically made by children learning their first language at the second stage in the development of negation. Cancino (1976), studying use of forms of the possessive by Marta, a five-year-old Spanish speaker learning English, found that in the early weeks Marta used the Spanish *de,* meaning *of* as her only possessive form. This is an interference error. Later on Marta stopped using *de* and began using *of* and *s,* the English possessive forms.

There is one way in which second language learners cope that error analysis cannot reveal, and that is avoidance of troublesome constructions. Through contrastive analysis we can predict which constructions will be difficult in a second language. For example Russian does not have the definite article. It is hard for anyone who did not learn English as a child to become competent in the use of this construction. I have known a Russian who solved the problem of the article by always placing it before nouns. He would say,

9. I am going to the Widener.

instead of,

9a. I am going to Widener library.

or,

9b. I am going to the library.

The use of constructions requiring the definite article cannot be avoided, but the passive voice, relative clauses, and other difficult constructions can and, according to Hakuta and Cancino, are avoided by speakers whose native language did not have the construction.

BILINGUAL EDUCATION

The question whether bilingual education should be provided through the public school system in the United States requires several different answers. The answer is yes if the prospective students are fluent in English, want to become fluent in a second language, and the bilingual program does not impose such a strain on the school budget that school programs of greater interest and concern in the community cannot be carried out. But, for the most part, these are not the circumstances in which bilingual education is being advocated today. Bilingual education is being proposed or offered because the prospective students have little or no command of English and a tenuous grasp of their native language. The most significant group of such children in the United States in the early 1980s are the native Spanish speakers in the Southwest. It is proposed that these children be educated in Spanish at the same time that they are being taught English, until their English is sufficiently fluent that their education can be continued in English; in this way they will become fluent in both Spanish and English. Supporters of this program of bilingual education think that achieving fluency in Spanish is extremely important for the Spanish speakers whose command of Spanish is limited in that they then will have a native language in which they are fluent. Proponents of the program believe that if these children are taught solely in English they will become fluent slowly or perhaps not at all and will not become educated; they will not learn the skills and acquire the knowledge that schooling should provide. If the arguments of the program's proponents are correct, they are compelling reasons to provide this kind of bilingual education. The need for the program arises because of this group's difficulty in becoming culturally assimilated or integrated in the United States. Some, or all, of the barriers previously discussed exist in the Southwest, and the consequence is the observed difficulty of the Spanish speakers in learning English. Where psychological and social barriers do not exist, nonnative English speaking children can be taught directly in English. If they begin their American education as kindergartners, they become sufficiently fluent in English by first grade that they are ready to learn to read.

Many language communities support after school programs that maintain the native language of the community in the children and foster their literacy in it. In the Boston area there are after school programs in Chinese, Greek, and Hebrew, for example. This kind of bilingual education gives the child the benefit of being educated in the language of the political-social community in which he or she lives, has citizenship, and in which the economic and intellectual life of the country is carried on. At the same time cultural heritage is made available as part of the child's education through the after school native language and culture programs.

Appendix:
Loveland's Test for Proficiency
in English and French

The material in this appendix has been excerpted from Shirley Loveland's study, *Some Aspects of Second Language Learning in Young Children: A Study of the Acquisition of Negation in English,* 1974.

TEST IN ENGLISH

Introduction

Do you remember the game about the little boy who always said no? No matter what his mother or his friends said to him, he always said no. Now I'll tell you some more things and you tell me what he said.

When his mother said, "Please eat your carrots," he said, "No, I won't eat my carrots." (Tester encourages child to join in on this response, not counted in score.)

Test Questions and
Expected Responses

1. When his friend said, "That's a jet," he said, "No, that's not a jet."
2. His mother said, "Are you asleep?" and he said, "No, I'm not asleep."
3. His friend said, "Have you ever been to Montreal?" and he said, "No, I've never been to Montreal."
4. His grandmother said, "You're a good boy," and he said, "No, I'm not a good boy."
5. His teacher said, "Do you want to paint?" and he said, "No, I don't want to paint."
6. His friend said, "I can climb that tree," and he said, "No, you can't climb that tree."
7. A man knocked at the door and said, "Is anybody home?" and he said, "No, there's nobody home."

8. His daddy said, "There's something in my pocket," and he said, "No, there's nothing in your pocket."

He always said, "No!"

TEST IN FRENCH

Introduction

Te rappelles-tu du jeu du petit garçon qui disait toujours non? Quelquefois il le disait en français.

Quand sa maman lui disait, "Mange tes carottes, s'il te plait." il disait, "Non, je ne mangerai pas mes carottes." (Les enfants doivent le dire avec la maitresse.)

Test Questions and Expected Responses

1. Quand son ami lui disait, "Ca, c'est un jet," il disait, "Non, ce n'est pas un jet."
2. Sa maman disait, "Dors-tu?" et il disait, "Non, je ne dors pas."
3. Son ami disait, "As-tu deja été a Montreal?" et il disait, "Non, je n'ai jamais été a Montreal."
4. Sa grandmere disait, "Tu es un bon garçon," et il disait, "Non, je ne suis pas un bon garçon."
5. Sa maitresse d'école disait, "Veux-tu peinturer?" et il disait, "Non, je ne veux pas peinturer."
6. Son ami disait, "Je peux grimper dans cet arbre," et il disait, "Non, tu ne peux pas grimper dans cet arbre."
7. Un monsieur a frappé à sa porte et a dit, "Y-a-t-il quelqu'un ici?" et il a dit, "Non, il n'y a personne ici."
8. Son papa disait, "Il y a quelque chose dans ma poche," et il disait, "Non il n'y a rien dans ta poche."

Il a toujours dit, "Non!"

SCORING OF CHILDREN'S ENGLISH AND FRENCH PROFICIENCY

Proficiency was scored solely in terms of percentage of Stage 3 responses in each language. Sentences (1), (2), (3), (4), (7), and (8) in English required Stage 3 responses. Sentences (1), (2), (3), and (4) require proficiency with the verbal auxiliaries *is am,* and *have.* Sentences (7) and (8) require the negative pronouns *nobody* and *nothing.* Sentences (3), (7), and (8) in French require the Stage 3 negatives *jamais, personne,* and *rien.*

12

Sociolinguistics

This final chapter provides a brief consideration of sociolinguistics, the study of language as a social behavior affected by variables like the sex, age, and social status of persons in verbal communication with each other. As a social behavior, language use is also influenced by social class, membership, ethnicity, and the changing customs and values of language users.

POLITENESS MARKERS

Suppose that you heard a business-like but pleasant male voice coming from an office with its door partly closed so you could not see the speaker or the person(s) to whom he was speaking. You heard the voice say,

1. Get ready to take a letter, Mary.

and several minutes later,

2. Would you mind taking this letter of mine down to the mail room when you take yours down?

Could you guess who was being addressed in (1) and (2)? There is reason to believe that different persons were being addressed in the two cases because (1) lacks the politeness markers that (2) has. A business man might address (1) to his secretary, and she might reply,

3. Yes, Mr. Jones.

If the response to (2) is,

4. No problem, Chuck.

regardless of whether the voice responding is that of a man or a woman, *the status relationships* of Chuck Jones to the person responding with (3) and with (4) are quite different. There are tell-tale signs of the difference in the language used in the two interchanges. I have mentioned politeness markers; the other sign is the use of first names (or nicknames) as opposed to Ms. and Mr. plus last name.

The situations in which politeness markers are most likely to be significant because of their presence or absence are just those of (1) and (2). One person wants a second person to do something for the first person. "Get ready to take a letter" is an *imperative,* a syntactive sentence form in English and other languages. Using the imperative form is expressing what you want done as an order or directive. Parents do this with their children. "Wash your hands," "Clean up your room," "come to supper," "stop that" are all imperatives frequently directed at children. And children speak this way to each other—"Get out of my way," "Help me," "Run faster," "Catch the ball."

It is offensive to adults to be addressed in the way an adult might address a child. Who does it to whom and why is it tolerated? The imperative form is used by persons of higher status and greater power when addressing persons of lower status and less power. Imperatives seem to be used less frequently now than a generation ago. It would make an interesting study of the United States' changing social customs and beliefs reflected in language to chart the history of imperative use to request behavior of another person. I cannot provide the history of the development of polite ways of guiding other people's behavior; instead I will give a brief analysis of the change.

HOW AND WHY
THE IMPERATIVE BECOMES POLITE

The imperative is the form of command. It's use indicates that the user expects to be obeyed. When Father says, "Stop that," or the commanding officer says, "Halt," they expect the persons addressed to do as they are told. Their expectation is based on their having the power to control the behavior of the persons addressed.

5. Would you mind mailing my letter?
6. Could you please mail my letter?
7. If it's not out of your way, would you mail my letter?

Each of these implies that the control of his or her behavior is in the hands of the addressee. For the most part, this is true of adults in the United States, but there are exceptions. Soldiers have to obey their commanding officer, and if a policeman says to a person, "Pull over," "Get in (the police car)," "Hand it over (the gun)," the person typically does as he or she is told. Commanding officers and policemen can back up their imperatives with the power to compel obedience. Furthermore they do not view themselves as being in a friendly relationship to the person they are ordering around that will be spoiled by their imperatives.

Politeness markers get attached to imperatives because, in many instances, the person requesting behavior does not have the power to compel it; therefore, phrasing a request in a way that acknowledges that the addressee is in control of his or her own behavior is appropriate and reflects the social reality of the situation. But even in the instances where there is considerable inequality in power, politeness markers may be in evidence to foster a spirit of friendliness and cooperation. People respond differently when they are treated as equals than when treated as inferiors.

In the United States we have a democracy, and the idea that some people are powerful enough to control the behavior of other people is repugnant to us. Language use reflects the values of the speech community, and in the United States polite forms of the directive are preferred to the imperative, not just in adult-adult interchanges but also when adults are speaking to children. For example, teachers say, "Do you want to collect the papers?"; "Can you shut the door?"; "Please pass the books in." "Please," "can you," and "do you want to" are ways of introducing a requested behavior while implying that the child has control over his or her behavior and could answer no rather than comply. Until rather recently in human history the law has been that children are under the control of their parents and do not have the same rights as adults. It was possible for parents to behave with impunity toward their children in ways that would get them put in jail if the behavior were directed at someone outside their family. An adult may take a switch or a belt to his or her child. If the same adult hit another adult with a belt, he or she could be arrested for assault and battery. Language use is an interpersonal behavior, and it will be consistent with other interpersonal behaviors. Socially appropriate language use is determined by the social beliefs and conventions of society. *Sociolinguistics* is the study of the relationship between power relationships, values, and social beliefs of a society and language use in the society. The effects of the variables, social status, age, and sex on language use have been widely studied. Power differences are implicated in the effect of each. Social interaction between persons of high and low social status, older and younger persons, and a man and woman typically reflect the dominance-submission relationship between the higher status, the older person, or the male and the lower status, the younger person, or the female. Since the 1970s the male-female interaction has been one of increasing equality.

THE EFFECT OF SOCIAL CLASS
ON LANGUAGE USE IN SCHOOLS

It has been proposed that the use of the imperative to direct or guide behavior is linked to social class. (Basil Bernstein 1976) Specifically, Bernstein, a British sociologist, has stated that the frequent use of short commands, that is, simple imperatives, is one of the features that characterizes lower socioeconomic status (SES) language use. The public school in the United States is predominantly a middle-class institution; American teachers and administrators in the latter part of the twentieth century are primarily from middle SES backgrounds and have been educated in the colleges of the United States, which are also predominantly middle-class institutions. There is a preference on the part of middle SES persons not to order other persons around, and this extends to the treatment of school children. This means not using simple imperatives to guide the children's behavior. In my observations of the interaction of preschool children and teachers, I have rarely heard a simple imperative from teacher to child except when there was immediate physical danger; even then, there typically followed an explanation of the danger and how the child was involved. "Come here, Bill," followed by, "That was a dangerous place to stand. Mary Ann's swing could have knocked you over," said a teacher as she and Bill watched Mary Ann's swinging. Usually children's behavior is guided by teachers' speech acts in which the behavior the teacher desires from the child is politely and indirectly specified. For example a preschool teacher said to a girl riding a tricycle, "Jean, it's about time to put the bikes away," meaning: put your bike away. To another child who was beginning to climb up the slide instead of going up by way of the steps, she said, "That's a one way slide," meaning: go up the steps. I think that children whose home experience has not included the use of politeness markers and indirect directives to guide their behavior may be confused by these in school. They may not understand that "Would you like to clean up, now" or "Isn't it about time to work on your spelling," mean "Do it," even though they sound as though they mean, "You decide."

A study of children's responses to questions about how they would get another child or their teacher to return something that belonged to them provides data on middle socioeconomic status children's use of directives (Montes 1978). The children were kindergartners and preschoolers, and first, second and third graders. They were interviewed individually to find out how they would get a person to return something that belonged to them. Most of the children would *say* something to get back their ruler or dog or whatever the object was. However, a few said they would grab it or use some other nonverbal means to secure the return of their paint brush or hammer. Montes categorizes the responses of the children who responded with a verbal means of getting back their property into direct, indirect, and inferred means. Direct and indirect correspond quite well to imperatives and to interrogatives that begin, "would you mind," "can you," and so on. The inferred category is made up of rights and reasons. Rights are responses based on ownership ("That's my pencil"), permission ("Teacher said I could keep the hammer till Monday"), and turntaking ("You've had your turn"). Reasons are responses like, "The longer you keep her (subject's dog), the hairier you'll get," the child said to his teacher to secure the return of his dog. The preschool examples, "It's about time to put the bikes away," and "That's a one way slide," would fall into the reasons category of this research and be inferred directives.

The middle SES children who were the subjects in Montes's research responded with a small percentage of direct directives (simple imperatives) as the means they would use in getting another person to return something that belonged to them. Since this was true for even the preschool and kindergarten children, it appears that avoiding the direct directive is learned in middle SES homes from the way the children's behavior is guided by their parents. Use of indirect and inferred directives seem to be about equally favored means for getting property returned. There are no comparable data for lower SES children to make a comparison of frequency of type of directive strategies. Thus I cannot say whether lower SES children would propose imperatives (direct directives) with greater frequency than middle SES children as implied by Basil Bernstein's theories. It should be remembered that Montes's research is not a naturalistic study of the actual use of directives by children but rather is a study of the frequency of directives the children *said to the experimenter* that they would use to get their property returned. It could be argued that all Table 12.1 tells us is that middle-class children as young as preschoolers know what the socially desirable directives are in an environment in which middle SES adult standards of politeness prevail. Actual behavior may differ from the socially desirable with a higher percentage of direct directives like "gimme back my doll" spoken than the children in this study say they would use. What may be crucially important is knowing what the socially desirable directives are so that, when the teacher says, "Do you want to pick up the crayons?" the child spoken to knows what is expected of him or her. Will lower SES children know this?

I have some evidence that leads me to say that they will. In doing a study

TABLE 12.1. Frequency Percent of Directive Strategies by Type and by Grade

	GRADE				
	PS	K	1	2	3
Direct	9	13	4	16	15
Indirect	36	48	56	43	31
Inferred	54	39	37	37	52
Total children	78	80	111	110	85

Montes 1978

of middle and lower SES children and mothers called "The verbal environment provided by mothers for their very young children" (1974) I found no class-linked differences in use of indirect, inferred, and direct directives. But I had only two mother-child pairs representing each class.

I have more compelling indirect evidence that lower SES children may not have had the home experience necessary to understand indirect and inferred directives. In a comparative study of language use by white, lower SES and middle SES preschoolers, Landau (1970) found significant differences in language use by the two groups of children. Landau studied 13 matched pairs of children, seven female and six male pairs, each pair matched on IQ (Stanford-Binet) and age. IQs ranged from 100-130, ages from three years and four months, to five years and one month. There were no significant mean differences in sex, age, or IQ between the middle and lower SES groups. The lower SES preschoolers had been in a suburban Head Start program in Massachusetts and the middle SES preschoolers in a university-affiliated preschool in the same geographic area. Landau obtained a 20 minute spontaneous speech sample from each child, sampled across the variety of free activity periods in each class. Samples were taped and hand recorded by Landau. She states that she had been the assistant teacher in the Head Start group all year so that whatever inhibition young children experience from the presence of a strange adult in their classroom would have affected the middle SES rather than lower SES children.

Landau's findings comparing characteristics of the children's spontaneous speech are presented in Table 12.2. Even though the children are matched for age, sex, and IQ, middle SES children's spontaneous speech is more complex and better developed than that of lower SES children. Middle SES children's syntactic development, measured using a method similar to Loveland's (Chapter Eleven), is also in advance of that of lower SES children.

Landau attributes her findings mainly to differences in maternal behavior and in home environment. Landau was able to observe the

TABLE 12.2. Spontaneous Speech: Characteristics of Lower and Middle SES Preschoolers

	Lower SES	Middle SES	Significance level
Number of responses	63	70	ns
Number of words	241	297	.05
Mean of five longest responses (number of words)	8	9	.02
Number of prepositions, adverbs and adjectives	21	27	.05
Number of personal pronouns	34	40	ns
Number of complex sentences	4	7	.02

Landau 1970

interaction of middle SES mothers and children when mothers picked their children up from preschool at noon. Mothers greeted children, asked what they had done at school, and talked about afternoon plans. Landau observed lower SES mothers as they took turns helping out in the Head Start class. "Even though mothers were supposed to be helping with the whole group, they primarily watched their own child's behavior and verbally jumped on him if he made a movement unacceptable to the mother, even though it was permitted by the teacher. Giving no explanation, a mother would say 'Stop it,' or 'Be quiet,' " (Landau 1970, p. 38).

Landau was unable to visit any middle SES homes, but I think we can go along with her assumption that the middle SES homes would provide better settings for language development than the lower SES homes. In the lower SES homes she visited, Landau noticed "an unusually high noise level. These homes were in a housing project and, in addition to a lot of noise in each apartment (that of television, many siblings, birds and other animals), there was a tremendous noise level from the neighboring apartments and the street outside. In general, there appeared to be at least one argument of some sort sifting in through the walls or windows," (ibid., p. 37).

In my judgment, the differences Landau found in mother-child interaction and noise levels of the homes, which adversely effected language use by her sample lower SES children, would also interfere with learning about indirect and inferred directives. It is not SES itself but the quality of experience that fosters or impedes development of language use. Experience in school with indirect and inferred directives, with time, will bring about their understanding by children who have not had experience with them at home. But initially lack of understanding contributes to the feeling of not being at home in the strange, new world of school.

In my home we kept up the custom of my German speaking ancestors of saying "Gesundheit" (to your health) to a person who had sneezed. The person would respond with "Dankeschöen" (thank you). When I started kindergarten, I rapidly found out that nobody except me said "Gesundheit" and "Dankeschöen," and I assumed that nobody said "please" and "thank you" either. This is another difference in language use, not SES linked, but linked to ethnicity, a complex of linguistic and cultural traditions related to one's "roots," or the origin of one's family. The group in the United States about whom there has been considerable research related to ethnicity are lower SES Blacks whose nonschool language is Black English, a systematic, grammatical, nonstandard English. Should Black English be the medium of education for children whose nonschool language is Black English? The pros and cons result from reasoning similar to that in the debates about bilingual education for Hispanics in the Southwest. The same patterns of discrimination, poverty, and conflicting values beset the lower SES Blacks and Hispánics. In neither case is there a consensus about what will be in the best interests of the children as far as language and schooling is concerned.

TERMS OF ADDRESS

Another way of studying how power relationships and societal values are reflected in language use is to look at terms of address, or the way people address each other, touched on at the beginning of this chapter.

If, for example, you read in a novel that a nine-year-old girl said to a grown man,

5. Fetch me my coat, Jim.

and the grown man answered,

6. Yes, Missy Angela.

you can figure out that Jim is a servant in a household in which Missy Angela is a child in the family that Jim serves. Further, the interchange took place in a highly stratified society in which the social gap between servant and master's family was wide and carefully respected. We can infer a great deal about a society and social relations in general from language use. In the examples discussed, (1), (2), (3), (4), and (5), and (6) we can see how power and social status relationships can be observed on the basis of the use of politeness markers and terms of address in verbal interaction. French, German, and Italian, among other languages, have both a familiar and a formal version of the pronoun that corresponds to *you* (singular). In French these are *tu*, familiar, and *vous* (used to address one person), formal. Brown and Gilman (1970) have made a study of the use of the familiar and formal pronouns by speakers of the three languages. There are three different possibilities:

1. Persons exchange the formal pronoun (reciprocal use).
2. Persons exchange the familiar pronoun (reciprocal use).
3. One person uses the familiar to the other person who returns the formal pronoun (nonreciprocal use).

We can see these same patterns in English in the use of a title (Mr., Ms., and so on) plus last name, corresponding to the formal, and first names, corresponding to the familiar.

4. Persons call each other by title plus last name (reciprocal use).
5. Persons call each other by first names (reciprocal use).
6. One person calls the other by title plus last name and is called by first name in return (nonreciprocal use).

For developmental psycholinguists, it is interesting to observe how language use by upper-class and lower-class males in conversation with one another mirrors language use by adults and children involved in discourse with each other. That is, prior to the 1960s newly acquainted adults or adults who had only business dealings addressed each other with title plus last name; children addressed each other with first names. Adults addressed children with first names, and children addressed adults with title plus last name. There has been a relaxation of the formality of address among adults, particularly younger adults, in the United States since the late 1960s so that a large proportion of the adult population expects to be on a first name basis with other adults. In this relaxation of formality in address among adults, we see how social change brings about change in language use. The disillusionment of the American people with the Vietnam war manifested itself, in part, in an abandonment of former standards of appropriate formality of dress and behavior, including language usage. This change was not uniform throughout the society. Some people adhered to old standards, but throughout the 1970s and into the 1980s it was possible to go to a theatrical or musical performance in the most prestigious theatre or concert hall in the large cities of the eastern United States and see some people in formal dress and others, male and female, probably young, informally attired, some even wearing jeans. It was no longer necessary when going to the opera to "dress up," and along with relaxation of the dress code came relaxation of the sociolinguistic code.

Relaxation of the sociolinguistic code in France began with the French Revolution. The nonreciprocal use of *tu* and *vous* was not consistent with the "égalité" (equality) of the revolutionary motto, nor reciprocal use of *vous* with "fraternité" (brotherhood) and for awhile universal use of *tu* was advocated. This usage did not continue long after the Revolution, and the prerevolutionary pattern of usage again became prevalent until well into the nineteenth century when, once again, nonreciprocal use of *tu* and *vous* began to give away to reciprocal use of *vous* between people who did not have affiliative relationships, and reciprocal use of *tu* for those who did. The same general trend in usage was true for German and Italian. Brown and Gilman feel that once usage becomes largely reciprocal, there is a tendency for the scope of reciprocal use of familiar address to expand at the expense of mutual use of the formal. Does this mean that eventually all speakers of languages with a familiar and a formal *you* will abandon the formal, or perhaps abandon the familiar form as has actually happened with *thee* and *thou,* the archaic, familiar, nominative and accusative forms of *you* in English? A student of historical linguistics might want to venture a response to the question.

SEX AS A SOCIOLINGUISTIC VARIABLE

Language use in English and many other languages has had a pervasive sexist bias. We have been known as *mankind* rather than *humankind* over the centuries. Our language is so locked into sexist usage that we have to consciously avoid the pronouns *he, his,* and *him* in referring back to an unspecified human being—*the baby, the child, the adult.* We say automatically, "When the child starts school, *he* may miss his afternoon nap." Since the 1970s we have become increasingly sensitive to sexist language; *mankind* has become *humankind,* chairmen have become *chairpersons,* and in the psycholinguistic literature, many writers consistently use *she* and *her* where *he, his,* and *him* would formerly have been used. In addition to the bias resulting from referring to human beings as mankind, vocabulary, grammars, and style of discourse have female and male characteristics, which may be given sexist interpretations. Vocabulary reflects differences between the man's world and the woman's world, or more prosaically, differences in female and male vocabularies are reflections of differences in sex roles, occupations, and interests. We might be surprised to hear a man call his 12-year-old son, "honey" or even "hon." It's alright for a father to call his baby boy, "honey," but some people might worry that a father's use of "honey" to a 12-year-old son might interfere with the son's developing manliness. It's all right for mothers to call their sons "honey" because it's a cross-sex relationship, and in this relationship males may continue to be called "honey" all their lives. In years past we would have expected women's vocabularies to be replete with cooking, sewing, child rearing, and housekeeping terms. As Conklin (1978) points out, a man whose vocabulary has a large complement of any of these sets of terms will be assumed to be a professional in the field. If he has a large cooking vocabulary, he must be a chef; a large child-rearing vocabulary, a pediatrician. Until the 1970s women, for the most part, were not professionals, and thus a large complement of profession-related terms in a woman's vocabulary would be unexpected and perhaps viewed negatively as unwomanly. In the 1980s women have come into the work force in a wide variety of occupations, so their vocabularies are no longer sexually marked by the absence of a component of occupation-related terms. Concommitantly, it has become more acceptable for men to be interested in cooking and other homemaking skills, and there is no longer the expectation of a strong sex-linked difference in men's and women's vocabularies, at least among younger adults in the United States. Lifestyles and values for both sexes have become more androgenous (having both female and male characteristics). To the extent that the trend toward androgeny persists in young people, it will be passed on to their children who will be told as part of family history that their grandfathers did not know how to cook and clean house and their grandmothers did not work outside the home. The vocabularies of female and male persons will no longer be strongly sex-linked.

Along with vocabulary differences, Lakoff (1973) reported differences in syntactic style between women and men. She wrote that women use *tag questions,* such as

1a. It's a dirty trick, isn't it?

or hedges,

1b. I think it's a dirty trick.

where a man would take full responsibility for the judgment,

1c. It's a dirty trick.

A woman would be more likely to use the subjunctive mood,

2a. I *would like* some supper.

where a man would say,

2b. I *want* some supper.

A woman might even phrase the request,

2c. I would like a little supper.

and a man might say,

2d. I want my supper.

The female syntactic style is more polite and tentative and less confrontational or assured than the male style. It has been suggested that feminine speech characteristics may stand in the way of the professional woman (Conklin). They may make her appear less competent and less sure of herself than a man. Here is an interesting question for systematic research. Tape recorders are so commonly used at conferences and executive meetings in government, business, and at professional conventions that it should be possible to collect samples of the speech of female and male participants for analysis of vocabulary and syntactic style.

LANGUAGE AS AN INDICATOR OF SOCIAL CLASS

There is one last topic, language and social class, to consider before concluding this chapter and book. The topic is explored in an interesting and entertaining way in the musical, *My Fair Lady,* and the play, *Pygmalion,* by George Bernard Shaw, on which the musical is based. Eliza Doolittle's Cockney accent marks her as a member of the lower class of London, England. In order to rise above her humble origins, Eliza must get rid of her cockney accent in favor of the accent of upper-class London. If she speaks in the accent of upper-class London, she will be taken for a member of upper-class society. This is shown to be true in the scene in which Eliza, in her newly acquired but perfectly functioning upper-class accent, says at an upper-class gathering, "But it's my belief they done the old woman in." What she says is interpreted by her hearers as the latest slang and judged by a young woman to be delightful. The young woman's mother says that she "really cannot get used to the new ways."

I can remember from my childhood in Denver, Colorado, prior to World War II a concern with speaking correct English that seems to have been absent since the 1960s. The speech code has gone the way of the dress code. In my childhood swearing was not considered a male speech habit, it was a lower-class, "probably" male behavior. There were usages in addition to swearing that marked lower-class speech, for example, use of the nonstandard negative contraction *ain't*. People who did not want to be considered lower-class did not say *ain't*. More generally, good grammar and correct pronunciation of words were important in establishing one's middle-class credentials. A great deal of time in public schools was devoted to the study of grammar, and in Denver children had elocution lessons in which they would recite such "pieces" as Lincoln's Gettysburg address to improve diction. One heard and was scornful of what linguists call *hypercorrection*. In order to avoid a particular grammatical error like saying *It's me* instead of *it's I* or *It's him* instead of *it's he*, the hypercorrecter overgeneralized a rule (for example, the rule that the nominative form of pronoun is used in a verb phrase if the verb is a form of to be) and made an error. The hypercorrecter says, "John gave the artichoke *to my father and I*," which should be "to my father and me" because *me* rather than *I* is the *accusative form* of this pronoun and is used following a preposition.

Today, judging by the speech and written work of my students and the speech of the high school students in the western suburbs of Boston, very much middle-class neighborhoods, there has not been the kind of concern with students' language use as they grew up as there was in my childhood. Perhaps all the young people I see have middle-class credentials and do not worry about the extent to which their speech and writing are ungrammatical. I have to admit that I have not made a thorough analysis. Perhaps these young people do not care whether they are regarded as middle class or lower class. Class membership seems not to have the significance in the United States that it once had.

What we witnessed in the United States beginning in the latter years of the 1960s is a relaxation of a wide range of standards for behavior. At the same time there has been less emphasis on maintaining tight boundaries between groups defined by sex, social status, and age. These social developments have been accompanied by changes in language use. If the social pendulum swings back again toward more stratification and compartmentalization, the changes, again, will affect our use of language.

Glossary

Androgenous. Having both male and female characteristics.

Aphasia. Loss or impairment of the ability to use or understand speech.

Cognitive. Having to do with mental processes; knowing and thinking.

Comment. A verbalization that is a remark concerning a topic; a discourse as opposed to a syntactic category.

Conditioning. A procedure by which an individual is caused to produce (or refrain from) a behavior by the association of the behavior with a reward (positive reinforcement) if the behavior is being encouraged or with a punishment (negative reinforcement) if the behavior is being discouraged.

Corpora. Several collections of utterances.

Corpus. A collection of utterances.

Critical Period. A biologically determined period in which an organism is capable of acquiring a particular behavior. Certain aspects of human language appear to have to be acquired before puberty.

Discourse. A sequence of utterances by one or more persons in which communication of thought takes place in a more or less orderly way.

Gloss. Define, explain, provide a running commentary for.

Grammar. All the rules (phonological, semantic, and syntactic) for a language. Rule systems based on what speakers of a language do are called descriptive grammars.

Grammatical. Speech or writing in accord with the rules of the language.

Holophrase. One-word sentence.

Illocutionary Force. Utterer's meaning or what the person means by his or her utterance; the function of the utterance.

175

Linguistics. The study of language as a rule-governed system, including its rules governing speech sounds (phonological rules), sentence structure (syntactical rules), and use and meanings of words and sentences (pragmatic and semantic rules).

Linguistic Ellipsis. An utterance that leaves out some of the words necessary for a complete sentence, but which is linguistically well formed because the syntactically correct sentence can be constructed from the linguistic ellipsis and the preceding sentence in the discourse, using the rules of English grammar. Example:

1. previous utterance: I want a cookie.
2. linguistic ellipsis: I do too.
3. correct sentence based on (1) and (2):   I want a cookie too.

Mean Length of Utterance (MLU). The number of words per utterance for a group of utterances, for example, a sample of utterances by a two-year-old child. MLU is frequently used as an indicator of grammatical complexity of utterances because more grammatically complex utterances require more words than less grammatically complex utterances.

Morpheme. Smallest meaning-bearing unit in a language. In English the morpheme is usually a word, but suffixes like *ed* marking the past tense, (walk, walk*ed*) or the plural *s* (apple, apple*s*) are also morphemes.

Occasion Meaning. The circumstance or activity to which a particular verbalization becomes linked; for example *bye bye* becomes linked to leave-taking.

Orthographically. Spelled in the written (English) alphabet.

Performatives. Acts that are accomplished simply by saying the words appropriate to the occasion, as when a judge says to the prisoner at the conclusion of the trial, "I sentence you to ten years in prison."

Phonetic. Relating to speech sounds.

Phonemic. The speech sounds that are contrastive in a language. For example /lut/ and /rut/ are different words in English because /l/ and /r/ are different phonemes. Japanese does not have separate phonemes /l/ and /r/, so a native Japanese speaker hearing *loot* and *root* would not know from the sound of the words said, without clues provided by context, that they were different words.

Phonology. Having to do with the sound pattern of a language, its phonemic structure, and the stress and pitch patterns that mark its syntactic structure.

Presyntactic. Verbalizations that are not syntactically well formed (grammatically correct).

Proposition, Propositional Content. Specifies an idea, person, or object and makes a comment (says something) about it.

Psycholinguistics. Study of language as a psychological as well as linguistic topic.

Referential Meaning. A word or phrase has referential meaning if it names an object.

Reinforcement. The reward, in the case of positive reinforcement, or the punishment, for negative reinforcement, used to condition a behavior of an animal (including human beings).

Semantic. Having to do with the linguistic meaning of words and sentences.

Sociolinguistics. The study of language use as it is affected by variables that influence social behavior, such as sex, age, and social status.

Speech act. A way of analyzing verbalizations, which contrasts with linguistic analysis.

Syntactic Markers. 1. The variable parts of words, like suffixes, that indicate the plural of nouns, the past tense of regular verbs, and so on. 2. Order of words in a sentence that, in English for example, indicates which noun is the subject of the verb and which the object.

Syntactic-Semantic Meaning. The meaning of a sentence in the English language as opposed to utterer's meaning, or what the person means by his or her utterance; the function of the utterance.

Syntax. Syntax is the set of rules that determines the way linguistic units, like words, can be combined to produce other linguistic units, like noun phrases, verb phrases, and sentences.

Topic. Some languages do not have grammars whose basic unit is the sentence which requires a verb as English does. Well-formed utterances in these languages may not contain verbs. The linguistic unit in these languages analogous to subject in English—what the utterance is about—is called the topic.

Utterance. A word, or words spoken one after the other to form a group. An utterance is not necessarily syntactically well formed.

References

ADAMS, M. J., and A. COLLINS. "A schematheoretic view of reading," in *New Directions in Discourse Processing,* ed. R.O. Freedle. Norwood, NJ: Ablex, 1979.

ANDERSON, RICHARD. "The role of knowledge in reading comprehension." National Institute of Education, Reading Synthesis Meeting. Washington, D.C., Sept. 23-26, 1981.

ANGLIN, J. *Word, Object and Conceptual Development.* New York: Norton, 1977.

AUSTIN, J.L., *How to do Things with Words.* London: Oxford University Press, 1962.

BATES, E., L. CAMAIONI, and V. VOLTERRA. "The acquisition of performatives prior to speech," *Merrill-Palmer Quarterly,* 21 (1975), 205-26.

BERKO, J. "The child's learning of English morphology," *Word,* 14 (1958), 150-77, 1958.

BERKOFF, M. "Social communication in canids; evidence for the evolution of a stereotyped mammalian display," *Science,* 197 (1977), 1097-99.

BONNER, J.T. *The Evolution of Culture in Animals.* Princeton, NJ: Princeton University Press, 1980.

BOWLBY, J. *Attachment.* New York: Basic Books, 1969.

BRESNAM, J. "A realistic transformational grammar," in *Linguistic Theory and Psychological Reality,* eds. M. Halle, J. Bresnam and G. Miller. Cambridge, MA: M.I.T. Press, 1978.

BROWN, R. *A First Language, The Early Stages.* Cambridge, MA: Harvard University Press, 1973.

BROWN, R. *Psycholinguistics,* R. Brown. New York: The Free Press, 1970.

179

BROWN, R. "Introduction" in *Talking to Children: Language Input and Acquisition,* eds. C.E. Snow and C.A. Ferguson. Cambridge, England: Cambridge University Press, 1977.

BROWN, R. "Symbolic and syntactic capacities," *Philosophical Transactions of the Royal Society in London* 292 (1981), 197-204.

BROWN, ROGER and CAMILLE HANLON. "Derivational complexity and Order of Acquisition in Child Speech" in *Psycholinguistics* by Roger Brown. New York: The Free Press, 1970.

CAREY, SUSAN. "The child as word learner," in *Linguistic Theory and Psychological Reality,* eds. Morris Halle, Joan Bresnan, and George Miller. Cambridge, MA: M.I.T. Press, 1978.

CARRIER, J., and H. LEET. "Effect of context upon children's referential communication." Tufts University, Unpublished Paper, 1972.

CARTER, A.L. "The transformation of sensory-motor morphemes into words: A case study of the development of 'more' and 'mine,' " *Journal of Child Language,* 2 (1975), 233-50.

CHAFE, W. "Givenness, contrastiveness, definiteness, subjects and topics," in *Subject and Topic,* ed, C. Li. New York: Academic Press, 1976.

CHALL, JEAN. *Learning to Read: The Great Debate.* New York: McGraw-Hill Book Company, 1967.

CHOMSKY, N. *Aspects of the Theory of Syntax.* Cambridge, MA: M.I.T. Press, 1965.

CONKLIN, N.F. "The language of the majority," in *A Pluralistic Nation: The Language issue in the United States,* eds. M.A. Lowrie and N.F. Conklin. Rowley, MA: Newbury House, 1978.

CROSS, TONI G. "Mother's speech adjustments: the contribution of selected child listener variables," in *Talking to Children: Language Input and Acquisition,* eds. C.E. Snow and C.A. Ferguson. Cambridge, England: Cambridge University Press, 1977.

DENES, P., and E. PINSON. *The Speech Chain: The Physics and Biology of Spoken Language.* Garden City, NY: Anchor Press/Doubleday, 1973.

DEVILLIERS, J., and P. DEVILLIERS. *Language Acquisition.* Cambridge, MA: Harvard University Press, 1978.

DORE, J. "Cognition and communication in language acquisition and development," paper presented at Boston University, Boston University Conference on Language Development, 1978.

DORE, J. "A pragmatic description of early language development," *Journal of Psycholinguistic Research,* 3 (1974), 343-50.

DORE, J., B. FRANKLIN, R.I. MILLER, and A.L. RAMES. "Transitional Phenomena in early language acquisition," *Journal of Child Language,* 3 (1976), 13-28.

FERGUSON, C.A. "Baby talk as a simplified register," in *Talking to Children: Language Input and Acquisition,* eds. C.E. Snow and C.A. Ferguson. Cambridge, England: Cambridge University Press, 1977.

FROMKIN, V., and R. RODMAN. *An Introduction to Language* (2nd ed.). New York: Holt, Rinehart & Winston, 1978.

GARNICA, O.K. "Some prosodic and paralinguistic features of speech to young children," in *Talking to Children: Language Input and Acquisition,* eds. C.E. Snow and C.A. Ferguson. Cambridge, England: Cambridge University Press, 1977.

GOLDNER, JUDITH. *Four Mother-Infant Dyads: Turn Taking and the Role of Rising Intonation in Infant Language Acquisition.* Unpublished master's thesis, Tufts University, 1981.

GREENFIELD, P., and S. SMITH. *Structure of Communication in Early Language Development.* New York: Academic Press, 1976.

HAKUTA, KENJI. "Prefabricated patterns and the emergence of structure in second language acquisition," *Language Learning.* 24 (1975), 287-98.

HAKUTA, K., and H. CANCINO. "Trends in second language acquisition research," *Harvard Educational Review,* 47 (1977), 294-316.

HERRNSTEIN, R., D. LOVELAND, and C. CABLE. "Natural concepts in pigeons," *Journal of Experimental Psychology, Animal Behavior Processes,* 2 (1976), 285-311.

HOLZMAN, M. "Evidence for a reciprocal model of language development," (1983), unpublished.

HOLZMAN, M. "Ellipsis in discourse: implications for linguistic analysis by computer, the child's acquisition of language, and semantic theory," *Language and Speech,* 14 (1971), 86-98.

HOLZMAN, M. "The use of interrogative forms in the verbal interaction of three mothers and their children," *Journal of Psycholinguistic Research,* 1 (1973), 311-37.

HOLZMAN, M. "The verbal environment provided by mothers for their very young children," *Merrill-Palmer Quarterly,* 20 (1974), 31-42.

HOLZMAN, M. "Where is under: from memories of instances to abstract featural concepts," *Journal of Psycholinguistic Research,* 10 (1981), 421-39.

HOLZMAN, M., E. MASUR, L. FERRIER, J. GOLDNER, K. O'LEARY, and J. MORSE. "How the human infant becomes a language user." In process.

ITARD, J. *The Wild Boy of Aveyron.* New York: Appleton-Century-Crofts, 1962.

KELLER, HELEN. *The Story of My Life.* Reprint, New York: Dell, 1961.

KLIMA, E.S., and URSULA BELLUGI. "Syntactic regularities in the speech of children," in *Psycholinguistic Papers: The Proceedings of the 1966 Edinburgh Conference,* eds, J. Lyons and R.J. Wales. Edinburgh, Scotland: Edinburgh University Press, 1966.

LAKOFF, R. "Language and women's place," *Language and Society,* 2 (1973), 45-79.

LANDAU, D.E. *A Comparative Study of the Language Use of Matched Groups of Lower-*

Class and Middle-Class Preschool Children. Unpublished Master's Thesis, Tufts University, 1970.

LASHLEY, K. "In Search of the Engram," *Symposia of the Society for Experimental Biology, 4: Physiological Mechanisms in Animal Behavior.* London: Cambridge University Press, 1950.

LENNEBERG, E. *Biological Foundations of Language.* New York: John Wiley & Sons, 1967.

LI, CHARLES N., and SANDRA A. THOMPSON. "Subject and topic: A new typology of language" in *Subject and Topic,* ed. Charles N. Li. New York: Academic Press, 1976.

LIEBERMAN, PHILIP. *Language, Cognition and Evolution.* Cambridge, MA: Harvard University Press, in press.

LIMBER, J. "Language in child and chimp," *American Psychologist,* 32 (1977), 280-96.

LORENZ, K. *Man Meets Dog.* London: Methuen, 1954.

LOVELAND, SHIRLEY. *Some Aspects of Second Language Learning in Young Children: A Study of the Acquisition of Negation in English.* Unpublished Master's Thesis, Tufts Uiversity, 1974.

MARATSOS, M. "Nonegocentric communication abilities in preschool children," *Child Development,* 44, 697-701.

MARLER, P. "Organization, Communication and Graded Signals: The Chimpanzee and the Gorilla," in *Growing Points in Ethology,* eds. P.P.G. Bateson and R. A. Hinde. Cambridge, England: Cambridge University Press, 1976.

MARLER, P. "Specific distinctiveness in the communication signals of birds," *Behavior,* 11 (1957), 13-39.

MARSHALL, J.C. "The biology of communication in man and animals," in *New Horizons in Linguistics,* ed. J. Lyons. Hammondsworth, Middlesex, England: Penquin, 1970.

MASUR, E.F. "Preschool boys speech modifications: The effect of listeners' linguistic levels and conversational responsiveness," *Child Development,* 49 (1978), 924-28.

MOERK, E. "Differential analysis of language teaching," Unpublished Paper, 1981.

MOERK, E. "Relationships between parental input frequencies and children's language acquisition: A reanalysis of Brown's data," *Journal of Child Language,* 7 (1980), 105-18.

MONTES, ROSA. "Extending a Concept: Functioning Directively," in *Children's Functional Language and Education in the Early Years,* eds. P. Griffin and R. Shuy. Final report to the Carnegie Corporation of New York. Washington, D.C.: Center for Applied Linguistics, 1978.

MORAN, LOUIS. "Comparative Growth of Japanese and North American Cognitive Dictionaries," *Child Development,* 44 (1973), 862-69.

MORGAN, J., and E. NEWPORT. "The role of constituent structure in the induction of an artificial language." *Journal of Verbal Learning and Verbal Behavior,* 20 (1981), 67-85.

MORSE, JOANNE. *How Babies Use Words: A Short History of Early Utterances as Speech Acts.* Unpublished Master's Thesis, Tufts University, 1981.

NELSON, K. "Individual differences in language; implications for development and language," *Developmental Psychology,* 77 (1981), 170-87.

NELSON, K. "Structure and strategy in learning to talk." *Monographs of theSociety for Research in Child Development,* no. 149 (1973).

NEWSOME, JOHN. "Dialogue and Development," in *Action, Gesture, and Symbol,* ed. Andrew Lock. London: Academic Press, 1978.

PREMACK, A., and D. PREMACK. "Teaching language to an ape," *Scientific American,* 227 (1972), 92-100.

RICHARDS, M. "The biological and the social," in *Action, Gesture and Symbol,* ed. Andrew Lock. London: Academic Press, 1978.

ROSCH, ELEANOR. "On the internal structure of perceptual and semantic categories," in *Cognitive Development and the Acquisition of Language,* ed. T.E. Moore, New York: Academic Press, 1973.

ROSCH, ELEANOR, WAYNE GRAY, DAVID JOHNSON, and PENNY BOYES-BRAERN. "Basic objects in natural categories," *Cognitive Psychology,* 8 (1976), 382-439.

RUMELHART, D.E., and J.L. McCLELLAND. "An interactive activation model of context effects in letter perception: Part 2," *Psychological Review,* 89 (1982), 60-95.

SCHUMANN, JOHN. *The Pidginization Process: A Model for Second Language Acquisition.* Rowley, MA: Newbury House Publishers, 1978.

SEARLE, J. *Speech Acts.* Cambridge, England: Cambridge University Press,1969.

SEARLE, J. "What is a speech act?" in *Philosophy in America,* ed. M. Black. Ithaca, NY: Cornell University Press, 1965.

SHATZ, M. "The Relationship Between Cognitive Processes and the Development of Communication Skills," in *Nebraska Symposium on Motivation 1977,* ed. C. B. Keasey. Lincoln, NE: University of Nebraska Press, 1978.

SHATZ, M., and R. GELMAN. "The development of communication skills: modifications in the speech of young children as a function of the listener," *Monographs of the Society for Research in Child Development,* No. 152, 1973.

SHAW, G.B. *Pygmalion.* London: Constable and Co., 1916.

SHOTTER, JOHN. "The cultural context of communication studies: Theoretical and methodological issues," in *Action, Gesture and Symbol,* ed. Andrew Lock, London: Academic Press, 1978.

SNOW, C. "The development of conversation between mothers and babies," *Journal of Child Language* 4 (1977), 1-23.

SNOW, C. "Mother's speech to children learning language," *Child Development,* 43 (1972), 549-65.

TERRACE, H., et al. "Can an ape create a sentence," *Science,* 206 (1979), 891-903.

TINBERGEN, N. *The Study of Instinct.* London: Oxford University Press, 1951.

VAILLANCOURT, MONIQUE. "At what age do French speaking children begin using different kinds of negations in their language?" Tufts University, Unpublished Paper 1968.

VALTIN, R. "Deficiencies in research on reading deficiencies," in *Orthography, Reading and Dyslexia,* eds. J.F. Kavanagh and R.L. Venezky. Baltimore, MD: University Park Press, 1980.

VYGOTSKY, L.S. *Thought and Language.* Cambridge, MA: M.I.T. Press, 1962.

WEINSTEIN, R. "Comprehension is the key: Illinois reading center finds ways to help," *APA Monitor American Psychology Association,* Washington, D.C., January 1982.

WELLS, GORDON. "Apprenticeship in meaning," in *Children's Language* (Vol. 2), ed. K.E. Nelson, New York: Gardner Press, 1980.

WERNER, H., and E. KAPLAN. "The acquisition of word meanings: A developmental study," *Monographs of the Society for Research in Child Development.* 15, (1950).

WILSON, E.O. "Animal communication," *Scientific American* 227 (1972), 52-72.

WOLFF, P. "The natural history of crying and other vocalizations in early infancy," in *Determinants of Infant Behavior IV,* ed. B. M. Foss, London: Methuen, 1969.

Index